THE
COOKING
CLUB
COOKBOOK

THE
COOKING CLUB
COOKBOOK

SIX FRIENDS SHOW YOU HOW TO BAKE, BROIL, AND BOND

THE COOKING CLUB

KATHERINE FAUSSET

SHARON COHEN FREDMAN

REBECCA SAMPLE GERSTUNG

CYNTHIA HARRIS

LUCIA QUARTARARO

LISA SINGER

Photographs by Alexandra Rowley

Ⓥ

VILLARD NEW YORK

Villard Books is a registered trademark of Random House, Inc. Colophon is a trademark of Random House, Inc.

Library of Congress Cataloging-in-Publication Data

The Cooking Club cookbook : six friends show you how to bake, broil, and bond / The Cooking Club, Katherine Fausset . . . [et al.]

p.   cm.

ISBN 0-375-75968-9

I. Cookery.   2. Cookery, International.   3. Menus.

I. Fausset, Katherine.   II. Cooking Club.

TX714.C65436 2001

641.5—dc21   2001055927

Villard Books website address: www.villard.com

Printed in China on acid-free paper

2 4 6 8 9 7 5 3

FIRST EDITION

Jacket and book design by Cynthia Harris
Food and prop styling by Cynthia Harris

for our mothers

ACKNOWLEDGMENTS

A warm, oven-mitted thank you to everyone who helped cook this book up, in particular:

Robert Hammond, Henry and Francine Rowley, and **Debra Singer** for lending us their kitchens. The folks at **Judy at the Rink** for loaning us such lovely props. The staff at **Smiler's** for providing us a room of our own. Our overseas correspondents, **Lorenzo Ortona, Sheila Pierce,** and **Ornella Vincenzino,** for their stamp of authenticity. Our very own home-economics teacher, **Bonnie Gerstung,** for sharing her years of experience. Our foodie friends and trusted advisers: **Caryl and Richard Actis-Grande, Nicole Aragi, Risa Cohen, Rory Evans, Nicki Finkel, Harriet Fredman, Grace Goodyear, Gloria Loomis, Ryan McKnight, Alix McLean, Ann Patty, Ken Rockenbach,** and **Allison Rubenstein.**

Ken Fredman, Charlie Moran, and **Pieter Mulder** for last-minute grocery runs and witty on-location banter. Menu muse **Matthew Rauch** for his role as culinary consultant. **Steve Gerstung** for eating Mini-Me Mac and Cheese five nights in a row. **Stephen Wallis** for giving up Alexandra every weekend for a month. **Eleni Gage, Georgia Close,** and **Robb Riedel** for taking our secrets to the grave.

Our parents (for everything): **Janet and David Cohen, Kay and Roy Fausset, Alice and Jim Harris, Sally and Tony Quartararo, Polly and Lee Sample,** and **Florence and Gene Singer.**

The group that got the ball rolling: **Jenny Jacoby, Jenny Rosenstrach,** and **Hilary Black.** Our editor, **Pamela Cannon,** for her effort, enthusiasm, and expertise. And finally our agent, **Claudia Cross** at Sterling Lord, for her guidance, encouragement, and unwavering belief that this book was a recipe worth making.

contents

THE
COOKING
CLUB
COOKBOOK

TWO COOKING
CLUB NECESSITIES:
AMPLE TINFOIL AND
A SENSE OF HUMOR

EAT! the true cooking club story

WHO WE ARE AND HOW IT ALL BEGAN

Cooking in New York City is like driving—no one in their right mind does it. In this city, dinner at home requires only two ingredients: a phone and a drawer full of take-out menus. Mongolian at midnight? Not a problem. Cooking, on the other hand, involves trawling for elfin-sized groceries at your corner deli, boxing out an angry executive to nab the last bottle of soy sauce, and then lugging a shopping bag up four flights of stairs in a brownstone walk-up to an apartment that you can't afford anyway. Never mind that when you make it home, what's called a kitchen by realtors is often a Holly Hobbie oven in the corner of the living room, an alcove off the bedroom, or sometimes part of the bathroom. In the end, leaving the groceries by the fridge to meet friends at the new tapas bar on the ground floor of your building seems like a more appetizing option.

So, why would six young independent New York women join forces to form a modern-day Tupperware party? Well, legend has it that Cooking Club was conceived late one night at Le Cordon Bleu over a warm platter of *truites aux morilles.* In reality, it was the six of us at lunch, staring into wilted Au Bon Pain salads in plastic containers, pondering greener pastures. Since we were all in entry-level publishing jobs, lunch for us was a ritualistic escape from a morning of unjamming the Xerox machine and opening reader mail. During this lunch, the subject turned, as it often did, to food—foods we loved, foods we ate growing up, foods we *wished* we ate growing up. Slowly, an idea began to take shape: We could meet once a month to try new recipes and bond as we did best—over food.

Looking back, the idea wasn't entirely without precedent in our lives. Publishing's not a lucrative game, and we were at the bottom of its food chain. We couldn't afford to eat out or order in every night, even if we wanted to. Three of us shared a tiny apartment on the Upper West Side, and our closetlike bedrooms hinged on the quintessential apartment anomaly: a spacious galley kitchen (complete with a dishwasher) that was downright suburban in size. With a square window cut through the wall of the kitchen facing into the living room, the apartment cleverly allowed a continuous flow of conversation between the roommate in the kitchen making her dinner (cereal or pasta) and the roommates flopped on the couch. Three individual meals were eaten and prepared in intervals like tag-team potluck. While the meals were not inspired, the conversation was. This was our postgraduate family dinner, when we would catch up on newsworthy gossip. ("Your bed was still made this morning . . . start talking NOW.")

So, it's only natural that eventually we realized our dinnertime ritual was a recipe worth repeating. But the increasing demands of work and love lives made planning group get-togethers nearly impossible. Sitting in Au Bon Pain that day, someone suggested the perfect solution: We'd have a set-in-stone date the first Sunday of every month. Each person would have to prepare only one dish for the group dinner, a realistic goal. (We'd all had short stints in book clubs, and gave them up when we became overwhelmed by the all-too-familiar feeling of sitting in class without having done the homework.) Suddenly, we were all talking at once—Spanish night, crepe parties, could we master Indian cooking?

None of us really knew how to cook, but the idea of a regular meeting with close female buddies was reason enough to sign on. We congratulated ourselves, set a date, and Cooking Club was born.

The inaugural meeting went off without a hitch. Lucia made a winning Simon and Garfunkel chicken dish (with parsley, sage, rosemary, and thyme), and Sharon brought wine from the Finger Lakes. But when the second meeting was called to order in Becky's apartment, ironically located in the Hell's Kitchen neighborhood, we were not so lucky. We sat down to a dinner vaguely dubbed Autumn Harvest Night—a catastrophic menu that included pumpkin bisque, Middle Eastern couscous, and olive ravioli. Soon after that we unanimously decided that each meal must have an assigned theme—not only to inspire and unite the group but to prevent any future fusion confusion.

It's hard to believe that we've been meeting and eating for five years now. Too many cooks in the kitchen? Not in this group. The recipe that we got right the first time was our mix of good girlfriends. At the end of the weekend, having a group to consult on any matter of concerns—"Are these leather pants too tight?" or "Can someone proofread my résumé?"—has been the most rewarding part of Cooking Club. Our Sunday dinners have survived two weddings, countless boyfriends (good and bad), and at least fourteen job changes. We're not even assistants anymore—we finally have the careers that we longed for during the days we spent figuring out how to transfer calls on a six-line office phone. We've graduated to our own apartments and even cook for ourselves in them, and have learned that balancing not only the menu but our different personalities was like perfecting a great but tricky recipe. Finding a middle ground in both friendships and cooking has been part of the process, and much of the fun. And the results have been more satisfying than we could have imagined.

WE COOK SEPARATELY,
BECAUSE IT'S
EATING EN MASSE
THAT'S IMPORTANT

recipe for a cooking club

INGREDIENTS FOR GETTING STARTED

Whenever we tell friends that we have a cooking club, some laugh, but most quickly fire off a battery of questions about the ground rules of our Sunday night suppers. And as we've sat there relating the details of our meetings, meals, and mishaps, we've witnessed more than one friend distractedly begin searching her mental Rolodex for potential members to form her own group. We're proud to say that we've helped launch several other cooking clubs in the greater New York area. That's actually one of the reasons why we've written this book—to tell people how much fun it is to cook with your friends. It's tastier than a book club, less regimented than family dinner (you only have to eat all your vegetables if you want to), and it beats leftover pizza any day. Here, to help get you going, are answers to questions we're asked all the time.

WHEN AND HOW OFTEN SHOULD WE MEET? We've found that once a month is frequent enough to be regular without feeling like a chore. But if you want to get together more often and all clubmates are willing, then go for it. We like to meet on Sundays because it's the end of the weekend, which means there is less interference with exciting plans (with the added bonus of hearing the immediate recap of Katherine's hot Saturday night date). Plus, you have all day to cook. Not that you'll need it, but it's nice to know that you won't have to cram a slowly simmered stew into thirty minutes after work.

WHAT TIME OF DAY? Dinner makes the most sense to us, but you might want to shake things up with a brunch (see page 122), lunch, or midnight munch. Whatever meal you choose, plan on at least a half hour for stragglers (or Lisa) to show up. The only time Lisa hasn't shown up a half hour late was the Sunday we changed the time by thirty minutes and forgot to tell her. So, Lisa, we're meeting at seven now instead of seven-thirty *forever,* okay? (Note that while this is momentarily infuriating, when she unveils fifty hand-wrapped Vietnamese spring rolls or a perfect pinwheel strawberry tart, one bite and we forgive her, till next month.)

HOW MANY MEMBERS? We found six to be a great number because inevitably somebody's going to be out of town, or have some other shoddy excuse, which, while devastating, is less so when you know someone's still bringing dessert.

WHAT IS WINE DUTY? Wine Duty was invented because in addition to the person who's going to be out of town, there's also the person who will be out of town until Sunday night and is *soooo* sorry but just may not have time to do that asparagus terrine she's been talking up for a month over e-mail. It's the get-out-of-jail-free card because, frankly, there are times when cooking takes too long (see "The Quick Fix," page 98). The problem with Wine Duty for a Sunday meeting is that in New York liquor stores are closed, and by the time Wine Duty person remembers that, it's already Sunday, and she shows up empty-handed, but ready to eat. Abuse of Wine Duty hasn't been a problem, as a guilty culinary conscience usually results in overcompensation at the next meeting.

HOW DO WE SELECT MEMBERS? We admit it: There have been some Cooking Club casualties. We have lost members, usually due to geographical relocation or a simple lack of interest. Face it, some folks are as flaky as a Crisco piecrust, and you need to weed out the chaff from the wheat as soon as possible. A go-get-'em attitude is our only prerequisite, although you get extra points for having a dishwasher. Once you've got your group of eager cooks signed on, be ready to deal with the inevitable enthusiasm slump. At this point intense pressure and guilt are helpful to ensure attendance. Cynthia will be the first to tell you that she has yet to miss a single meeting.

WOULD WE DARE GO CO-ED? We've thought about it. But not for long. There's something to be said for sitting around in sweatpants and letting the topic of conversation jump from the leggy babe spotted fawning over a deadbeat ex at a bar the night before to what sample sales are cropping up in the week ahead to bachelorette party strategies for members with nuptials pending. There's been some interest in joining our club from those of the male persuasion. More than one boyfriend has attempted to gain entry under the title Guest Chef, and we even received a two-page manifesto outlining one amour's impressive credentials, along with something akin to a bribe. The unanimous decision, however, was thumbs down. We try to keep the boys' appearances limited to our Ho-Ho-Holiday Parties and Summer Soirees (see "Drinks Are on Us," page 146), which have become (in certain circles) very hot tickets indeed.

That said, one third of us are married now, and even wedded bliss can't keep those members home on CC nights, leaving their husbands alone and hungry. If you can't bear to blow off the boyfriend, we think a Couples Cooking Club could work just as well as the all-female variety. Just don't come crying to us if Mr. Right doesn't turn out to be your very own Naked Chef.

WHAT DO WE COOK? Think themes. Themes are fun. Themes get you excited to cook. They also mean that six or more dishes will probably work together. Plan menus and choose courses ahead of time over e-mail, by phone, or in person. This way you won't end up with six desserts. (On second thought, that might not be such a bad idea.) And though we don't have an official course rotation policy, we try to take turns preparing different parts of the meal. For convenience, we'll usually convene at the home of the member cooking the entrée, since carting a ten-pound turkey through a subway turnstile is no fun at all.

CAN VEGETARIANS AND CARNIVORES PEACEFULLY COEXIST? While we don't have any full-fledged vegetarians among us, we do have a club chock-full of picky eaters. The beauty of having multiple dishes and courses is that if one dish offends the delicate sensibilities of a clubmate, there's always something else to eat. You should be able to experiment with any and all foods, just no force-feeding. Don't think we haven't tried.

SO, HOW DO YOU DEAL WITH PICKY EATERS? Everybody has foods they don't like. But you can look at the idiosyncratic tastes of your clubmates as a nuisance or a challenge. No matter what, with enough time spent together you'll start to factor in your clubmates' likes and dislikes unconsciously. It's rather sweet, actually. But be ready for surprises. While most of us exposed our deepest food phobias right off the bat (Cynthia's aversion to oranges was announced day one), it wasn't until year four that Becky blurted out at brunch night, "Okay, that's IT! I HATE smoked salmon! Always have! HATE! HATE! HATE!" The philosophical question about whether a great cook must be open to all foods perplexed us for a moment, until Sharon imagined being locked up for eternity in a room full of olives and Lisa imagined mandatory milk consumption at every meal.

DO WE COOK TOGETHER? No. Prepare as much as possible in advance, separately, at home. Want to know why? Just try it the other way. Okay, believe us now? This rule came about as a function of necessity. With limited space in our New York City kitchens, we couldn't all fit in one kitchen if we wanted to, so we do everything but last-minute assembly at home. By cooking separately, we discovered that everyone gets the supreme feeling of accomplishment that they have created a dish all by themselves—and knows how to re-create it at a moment's notice. Cooking independently also helps develop the all-important Cooking Confidence—the strength to face the kitchen again even after your fruit-cake flops. And it's *eating* en masse that's important.

DO YOU HAVE TO BE A GOOD COOK? No. God, no! We're not naming names, but there were a few of us who had to relearn that hitting the defrost button on the microwave does not count as cooking, and that the question "Lucia, what's in your eggnog?" really shouldn't be answered with "Oh, a carton of eggnog and rum." The goal is not to be per-fect, but to be willing to try. Those of us who fantasized about an immediate Martha-morph were deflated like soufflé with our first aggressive attempts at something new. But as it turns out, mediocre okra can be a learning experience. This brings us to the final question:

WHY ARE WE DOING THIS? For FUN. Remember this. Repeat it like a mantra. Tem-pers run hot in the kitchen and egos can be bruised like a delicate persimmon. Be sensitive to your fellow clubmates' vulnerabilities. When Cynthia's handcrafted broccoli Christmas tree began to fall apart in large chunks at our holiday party, did we laugh? No. We ate up the branches when she was in the other room and hid the rest in the dip. Remember to boost the Cooking Confidence in one another as much as possible. When we meet, we spend the first ten minutes "mmm"ing and patting each other on the back. Mutual admira-tion and support is the name of the game. It's what will get you and the gang back into the kitchen month after month.

KILLER SANGRIA
AND MUSSELS IN
WHITE WINE AND
SAFFRON SAUCE

spanish

MENU

SPINACH AND CHORIZO
EMPANADAS

PATATAS BRAVAS

ALMENDRAS FRITAS
(FRIED SPANISH ALMONDS)

MUSSELS IN WHITE WINE
AND SAFFRON SAUCE

PEARS RIOJA

KILLER SANGRIA

oil of olé

GRINGA GIRLS RUN WITH THE BOWLS

Truth be told, Cooking Club got a little cocky. After a successful first few months, we were a well-oiled machine, each member churning out dishes with ease: a winning pesto sauce here, a flawless roast chicken there. We dined like queens, shared secrets, and toasted one great meal after another. This cooking thing, we decided, was a cinch.

But that was all about to change. One Sunday, after enjoying the fruits of an early CC success (featuring delicious dishes we'd all made before), ChefCyn, our fearless leader, organizational guru, and dumpling doyenne, issued us a challenge: no more familiar food. That meant ixnay on your mom's meatloaf that you'd mastered when you were eight. We'd venture into uncharted territory. We'd go international. And that didn't mean Tex-Mex.

Our initial culinary expedition was to Spain, despite, or perhaps precisely because of, the fact that we could barely come up with a signature Spanish dish. After an exhaustive debate we decided that Rice-A-Roni's Spanish rice did not qualify. No one had more than a working knowledge of Spanish 101. Tapas? Sure, but what were they? Spurred on by the invigorating breezes of a particularly balmy April, we set our sights on Iberia. We tapped all our resources: once and future roommates, *The New York Times* Travel section, our cookbook collections, good old Google.com, and, in a pride-swallowing instance, even an ex-boyfriend. Revitalized and ready to get our oven mitts dirty, we were determined to create an authentic fiesta.

To stay true to custom, we made a tapas feast, a bevy of appetizers that allowed us to sample a bit of everything. Patatas Bravas, or "Brave Potatoes," because they're spicy, is a common tapas dish whose recipe came to us through Becky's old roommate and man-of-honor in her wedding, Robb Riedel. Our savory Spinach and Chorizo Empanadas are a little on the spicy side, too. *Empanar* is Spanish for "to bake in pastry," so we did just that—we used Pillsbury piecrusts for the shells so that we could concentrate our efforts on perfecting the filling. (Or at least that's what Lucia told us.) Our recipe for Almendras Fritas, or Fried Spanish Almonds, is so easy, and packs such a delicious little punch that we really do find it impossible to eat just one. For the last tapas dish, we were tempted to try our hand at paella, but the cacophony of traditional ingredients—scallops, calamari, mussels, shrimp, clams, chicken, and rabbit—seemed overwhelming. (And, God forbid, we could never eat bunnies.) So instead, Sharon simplified things and focused on one ingredient, mussels. Her recipe features Spain's trademark spice, saffron, and is as pretty to look at as it is delicious to eat, if we do say so ourselves.

We washed down our Spanish spread with sangria, a Cooking Club favorite. Ours brims with citrus and is infused with fruit-flavored iced tea. And if you're looking for an attention-grabbing finish to your evening, try the Pears Rioja, poached pears in a red wine reduction. Douse them with rum and ignite for your guests—because there's nothing quite like an open flame for a real grand finale. Olé!

SPINACH AND CHORIZO EMPANADAS

This empanada is a variation of a *panata,* an Italian spinach pie served at Lucia's family Christmases. The recipe is so sacred and beloved, she wouldn't let us print it (to the relief of siblings and cousins on both coasts). Instead, Lucia turned its Italian roots Spanish by replacing bread dough with piecrust, and hot Italian sausage with Spanish chorizo. *Feliz Navidad,* everyone.
▪ *Yield: 2 large empanadas, which serve 8 to 10 as part of a tapas buffet*

¾ pound chorizo, cut into ½-inch cubes

2 cups chopped onions

1 clove garlic, chopped

5 tablespoons unsalted butter

1 10-ounce package frozen chopped spinach, thawed and drained

⅓ cup white wine

½ cup fresh parsley, minced

4 tablespoons plain breadcrumbs

½ teaspoon salt

½ teaspoon freshly ground black pepper

2 Pillsbury prepared piecrusts (dough available in the refrigerator section of your supermarket)

egg wash (1 egg beaten with 1 tablespoon water)

1   Preheat the oven to 375 degrees.

2   In the same skillet, fry the chorizo until cooked through and crispy on the outside. Set it aside and let it cool.

3   In a large skillet, cook the onions and garlic in the butter over medium-low heat, stirring occasionally, until soft. Squeeze out as much water as possible from the spinach, making sure to strain, then add to the onion mixture. Cook over moderate heat, stirring occasionally, until all the excess water from the spinach has evaporated.

4   Add the chorizo and the wine to the onion and spinach mixture and cook about 3 to 4 minutes, until the liquid has evaporated.

5   In a bowl, stir together the spinach and chorizo mixture, the parsley, and the breadcrumbs. Add salt and pepper and cool, uncovered.

6   Unfold the piecrusts and spread them out on a lightly floured surface. Spread half of the filling onto one half of one crust, leaving a half-inch border. Fold the other half of the crust over the filling, making a half-moon shape, and pinch the edges together. Cut 4 to 5 slits across the top of the empanada. Brush the top and edges with the egg wash. Repeat this process for the second empanada and place both on an ungreased pastry sheet.

7   Bake for about 30 minutes, or until golden brown. Let them cool completely, then slice them into 1-inch-wide pieces.

PATATAS BRAVAS

One Sunday, against Cooking Club custom, Becky brought her old roommate Robb to dinner. The extra guest—and the dish he made—were a ploy to distract us from the fact that Bec, experiencing the culinary equivalent of writer's block, happened to be on her third consecutive tour of Wine Duty. Robb's potatoes were so delicious that we forgave Becky—and kept Robb on retainer as an official consultant. You can find this typical tapas dish just about everywhere in Spain. It's rumored to have originated in Aragon, a province in the northeast, but it goes down in CC history as Becky's saving grace. ▪ *Yield: 8 to 10 servings as part of a tapas buffet*

4 large Idaho potatoes, peeled and cut into ½-inch cubes

¼ cup olive oil

salt to taste

1 clove garlic, minced

½ small Spanish onion, minced

1 cup water

1 teaspoon flour

2 tablespoons Tabasco

4 tablespoons tomato paste

1 bay leaf

1 teaspoon sugar

2 tablespoons red wine vinegar

SPANISH

1   Place the potatoes in a large pot and cover with water. Bring to a boil and cook for about 10 minutes, until tender. Drain and set aside.

2   Heat 2 tablespoons of the oil in a skillet over medium heat. Add the potatoes and sauté until golden brown and crispy on the edges, about 20 minutes. Remove the potatoes and sprinkle them with salt.

3   In a large skillet, sauté the garlic and onion in the remaining 2 tablespoons of oil over medium heat until they are transparent and soft. Add the water and the remaining ingredients and stir to combine. Cook down for 5 to 10 minutes. Remove the bay leaf and pour the sauce over the potatoes. Use toothpicks to serve.

ALMENDRAS FRITAS
(FRIED SPANISH ALMONDS)

There's a great Spanish restaurant on Crosby Street that serves these fried almonds, which we had one night while sipping sangria and watching flamenco dancers stomp and spin authoritatively in the packed bar. We're not positive we've nailed down the almonds, but they sure make us want to stomp and spin around in the kitchen. Not bad for a nut. • *Yield: 8 to 10 servings as part of a tapas buffet*

¼ cup olive oil
2 cups whole almonds
1 teaspoon ground cumin
1 tablespoon crushed red pepper flakes
1 teaspoon salt

1   Heat the oil in a skillet over medium-high heat. Stir in the almonds and cook until golden brown, about 3 to 4 minutes, flipping occasionally to brown both sides. Remove from the heat and strain.

2   Place the almonds in a mixing bowl and toss them together with the seasonings until well coated. Serve them warm, or let them cool and store them in a well-sealed container.

MUSSELS IN WHITE WINE
AND SAFFRON SAUCE

We knew we couldn't get away with writing about Spanish cuisine without including a recipe that featured saffron, the signature Spanish spice. Saffron, the stigma of the crocus flower, is prized for its deep yellow color and rich, if slightly bitter, flavor. It takes 225,000 handpicked stigmas to equal just a pound of saffron, making it the most expensive spice in the world. Savor these mussels. Dip a nice, crusty bread in the yellow broth and don't let a drop go to waste. We didn't. • *Yield: 6 to 8 servings as part of a tapas buffet*

2 tablespoons olive oil
1 cup chopped Spanish onions
3 cloves garlic, minced
1 teaspoon crushed red pepper flakes
1½ teaspoons saffron
1½ pounds mussels, washed and debearded
¾ cup white wine
1 cup tomatoes, diced
⅔ cup green olives, pitted and diced
juice from 1 lemon
2 tablespoons fresh parsley, chopped

1   Heat the oil in a skillet over medium-high heat. Add the onions and garlic and cook until slightly tender, stirring often, about 3 minutes. Stir in the crushed red pepper and the saffron.
2   Add the mussels, coating them evenly with the onion mixture. Add the wine, then cover the skillet. Let the mussels steam until they begin to open, about 5 minutes.
3   Reduce the heat to low. Gently stir in the tomatoes, olives, lemon juice, and parsley. Cook for an additional 5 minutes. Discard any unopened mussels before serving.

SPANISH

PEARS RIOJA

We like to flambé stuff. We have to admit, it's kind of exciting. When Lucia was growing up, her mom used to make this pear dish, and the flambé aspect spiced up the idea of having *pears* for dessert, a mundane prospect when things like Fudgsicles and Flying Saucers lurked in the freezer. Feel free to substitute another fruity red wine for the Rioja. ▪ *Yield: 6 to 8 servings as part of a tapas buffet*

½ cup red Rioja wine

¾ cup sugar

juice from 1 lemon

2 cinnamon sticks

¼ teaspoon nutmeg

4 pears, preferably unripened Bosc,
peeled, cored, and sliced into ¼-inch wedges

3 tablespoons rum

2 pints vanilla ice cream

I   In a medium saucepan, combine the wine, sugar, lemon juice, cinnamon, and nutmeg and bring to a boil, stirring occasionally. Reduce the heat.

2   Add a few pear slices at a time and cook for about 1 minute, or until slightly soft. Remove with a slotted spoon and set aside. Repeat until all the slices have been cooked.

3   Continue cooking the mixture until the sauce has been reduced by half and has thickened, about 5 to 10 minutes. Place the cooked pears in a skillet. Pour the rum into the skillet and ignite carefully. Let the mixture cook in the flames for a few seconds, then cover with a lid to extinguish. Serve the pears and sauce over vanilla ice cream. Remove the cinnamon sticks before serving.

A BRAVE FRIEND LENT US HIS
GARDEN APARTMENT FOR
SPANISH NIGHT SO WE COULD
SIP OUR SANGRIA IN STYLE

BECKY BREAKS BREAD FOR
SPANISH NIGHT, AS KATHERINE
AND LISA WONDER IF A SERRATED
KNIFE MIGHT MAKE IT EASIER

KILLER SANGRIA

This recipe needs no introduction. We love it. We drink it, a lot. That may be why we've tempered ours a little with fresh-brewed iced tea. It's very refreshing on a sticky summer night and is great for parties, too. Lemon tea will give your sangria a zippy, tart flavor, but other fruit-flavored teas, like wild berry or orange, are nice as well. Use your favorite. • *Yield: 2 quarts*

6 cups water
4 Lemon Zinger tea bags
2 tablespoons sugar (or to taste)
2 cups dry red wine
1 green apple, cored and thinly sliced lengthwise
1 orange, thinly sliced
1 lemon, thinly sliced
1 lime, thinly sliced

1   Bring the water to a boil in a medium saucepan, then remove from the heat. Add the tea bags and let steep for 2 to 3 minutes. Remove the tea bags and pour the tea into a large pitcher. Add the sugar and refrigerate for 1 hour.

2   Add the wine and fruit to the pitcher. Fill glasses with ice and serve.

SPANISH

mediterranean

MENU

EGGPLANT TZATZIKI

SPICED SQUASH SOUP

SALT-BAKED SALMON

ISRAELI COUSCOUS WITH
ARUGULA, TOMATO, AND FETA

BROCCOLI RABE WITH
GARLIC AND PINE NUTS

ITALIAN
STRAWBERRY TART

well feta

CRUISING THE MEDITERRANEAN FOR A SEA OF NEW FLAVORS

MEDITERRANEAN NIGHT TAKES SHAPE OVER E-MAIL:

sharon: after several late-night conference calls to the james beard institute, it's confirmed. our theme this month will be mediterranean!

cynthia: hooray! i'll bring my dandelion-print bikini and the bain de soleil.

katherine: is it just me or is *mediterranean* hard to spell? the ratio of *r*'s to *t*'s gets confusing, never mind the *e*'s and *a*'s.

becky: but you don't spell it . . . you eat it.

lisa: what did ralph fiennes eat in *the english patient*? was that in the mediterranean? what countries are we talking about here?

lucia: ralph fiennes . . . mmm.

After a brief Web search and a glimpse into how a fifth-grader today completes his homework, we were able to hurdle the first two obstacles to Mediterranean night. Online, we found a map of the Mediterranean Basin (spelling confirmed), and counted sixteen countries bordering those blue waters. (Extra credit if you can name two on the North African shoreline.) The next challenge was integrating all the flavors into our dinner, a task that required a fair amount of culinary diplomacy.

We consulted chefs, cookbooks, and cartographers, and decided the following regions were fair game: North Africa, the European arc, and a little bit of the Middle East. And just as dictators divided up World War II Poland by laying toothpicks end to end on a map, we divvied up the area, each of us acting as an attaché for a region—and a dish.

We began on the sea's eastern shore, with a bona fide Cooking Club invention—Eggplant Tzatziki. It's what happens when you cross the Middle Eastern dish baba ghanouj with the Greek dip tzatziki. Katherine riffed from a basic version of the Greek yogurt-and-cucumber dip and blended in a roasted eggplant. We gobbled up our newly minted hybrid with pita triangles, but it's also tasty with baby carrots.

Then, just like the Phoenicians, our taste buds sailed west to a North African Spiced Squash Soup. As with so many soups, this recipe is easy to prepare—and left us wondering why we don't make them more often. Cynthia's hankering for a Bain de Soleil tan prevailed, bringing us to the south of France. The Provençal dish Salt-Baked Salmon was a victory on many levels—not least of all the olfactory, which is no small consideration. In the average New York apartment, you'll smell whatever you've cooked—as well as whatever your neighbors have cooked—for the next three days. Because the salmon is baked on a dry bed of salt, there's no lingering fishy odor. We served the salmon on a bed of Israeli couscous, which is a supersized version of the regular kind. (It's almost orzolike.) The pearls of pasta absorbed the lemon and olive oil dressing, making it a summery complement to the fish. We tossed feta, arugula, and tomato into our couscous, but there are infinite ways to vary this recipe.

The boot of Italy stamped its way into our meal with Sharon's Broccoli Rabe with Garlic and Pine Nuts. It further proved the theory that if you add garlic and olive oil to vegetables, anyone will eat them. The recipe was based on a dish created by a Cooking Club member's former boyfriend. While the relationship ended before our clubmate could transcribe his recipe, it was, much like its original author, replaced with something even better.

For dessert, we served an Italian Strawberry Tart. Unlike a classic tart, this one doesn't have a rich, creamy filling, so it's light enough to eat while you're basking seaside in a chaise longue. For anyone planning a shindig of their own in the Mediterranean, our catering services are available. Our rates are particularly low on the Riviera.

EGGPLANT TZATZIKI

Since this recipe is a hybrid of the Middle Eastern eggplant dip baba ghanouj and the Greek yo-gurt dip tzatziki, we're thinking about branding it "babaziki." The best thing about this dip is that while baba ghanouj is typically made with tahini (sesame) spread—an addition that packs in a button-popping eighteen extra grams of fat—our yogurt-based dip is much less fattening. But we'll save the calorie-cutting for the spa chapter. ▪ *Yield: 4 to 6 servings*

1 medium eggplant (about 1½ pounds)
3 tablespoons plain nonfat yogurt
1 clove garlic, minced
1 tablespoon olive oil
½ cup cucumber, peeled, seeded, and diced
salt to taste
flat-leaf parsley, for garnish
pita bread, cut into triangles, for serving

1   Preheat the oven to 450 degrees.
2   Prick the eggplant all over with a fork. Place it on a foil-lined pan and roast it until it collapses and the skin turns brown, about 45 minutes. When done, set it aside to cool. After the eggplant has cooled, slice it in half lengthwise and scoop out the flesh into the bowl of a food processor. Add the yogurt and garlic. While running the food processor, drizzle in the olive oil. Stir in the cucumber and salt and garnish with parsley. Serve with pita triangles, baby carrots, or other crudités.

Note: This recipe can be prepared a day in advance. Add the cucumbers and garnish right before serving.

SPICED SQUASH SOUP

Butternut squash is apparently a serious player on the midwinter Mediterranean menu. We chose cinnamon, nutmeg, and cardamom to complement the squash's natural sweetness, but you could easily substitute curry powder, ginger, or ground cloves for the spices listed below. Serve this with warm focaccia for an easy weeknight dinner. ▪ *Yield: 4 to 6 servings*

2 tablespoons unsalted butter, melted

1 teaspoon cinnamon

½ teaspoon nutmeg

½ teaspoon cardamom

1 butternut squash, cut in half lengthwise and seeded

2 tablespoons olive oil

½ cup chopped onion

1 medium apple (such as McIntosh or Cortland),
peeled, cored, and chopped

3½ cups canned chicken broth

salt and fresh pepper to taste

chopped chives, for garnish

1 Preheat the oven to 425 degrees.

2 In a small bowl, combine the melted butter, cinnamon, nutmeg, and cardamom.

3 Place the squash halves flesh side up in a roasting pan. Prick the flesh several times with a fork, then spoon the spice-butter mixture evenly over both halves. (Pour any excess into the seed cavity.) Cover the pan with aluminum foil and bake for about 50 minutes, until the squash is tender.

4 In a soup pot, heat the olive oil over medium heat. Add the onion and apple and sauté until the onion is wilted and the apple is soft, about 10 minutes.

5 When the squash is done, scoop out the flesh and add it to the onion-apple mixture. Pour in the broth.

6 Transfer the soup in batches to a food processor or a blender and puree it until smooth. (If you have a hand-mixing "wand," you can puree it right in the pot.)

7 Return the soup to the pot. Add the salt and pepper. Bring the entire mixture to a boil, then simmer it for 5 minutes. Serve garnished with chives.

SALT-BAKED SALMON

This is a twist on a Mediterranean classic. The dish is traditionally made in the oven using a whole fish, with the head and tail intact. Not only is our version delicious, it doesn't stare back at you in an ominous way. You can average a half-pound of fish per person if you're serving this as a main dish. • *Yield: 4 to 6 servings*

2½ cups kosher salt

2 pounds salmon fillet, cut into 4 pieces

salt and white pepper to taste

about 10 to 12 sprigs fresh dill,
plus additional for garnish (optional)

1 lemon, cut into round slices,
plus additional for garnish (optional)

1   Pour the kosher salt into a large skillet. Heat over medium-high heat for 5 minutes.

2   Rinse the salmon fillets and pat them dry. Season them with salt and white pepper.

3   Place the salmon, flesh side up, on the salt bed. Top with the dill sprigs and lemon slices.

4   Cover the skillet and cook the fish for 12 to 15 minutes (depending on the thickness of the fillet), until the center of the thickest part is opaque. (Use a sharp, thin knife to test.) To serve, insert a spatula between the fish and the skin. Garnish with additional fresh dill and lemon slices if desired.

COOKING SALMON ON A DRY BED OF SALT MEANS THERE'S NO LINGERING FISHY SMELL TO FRIGHTEN LISA'S NEIGHBORS

ISRAELI COUSCOUS WITH ARUGULA, TOMATO, AND FETA

Israeli couscous seems to travel undercover. We've spotted it masquerading as Jerusalem couscous, Middle Eastern couscous, and even *couscous grande*. What you're looking for are small white balls—smaller than the size of a pea, but bigger than the grains of traditional couscous. If you can't track it down, this recipe works well with orzo pasta. (Follow the cooking time on the package to prepare the pasta.) ▪ *Yield: 4 to 6 servings*

1½ cups Israeli couscous

1 teaspoon kosher salt

3 cups water

juice from 1 lemon (about ⅓ cup)

⅓ cup olive oil

4 scallions, thinly sliced (white parts plus 2 inches of green)

1 bunch arugula, thinly sliced (about 2 cups)

1 pint grape tomatoes, halved (about 1½ cups cherry tomatoes
or diced plum tomatoes can be substituted)

¼ pound feta cheese, diced

¼ cup flat-leaf parsley, chopped

freshly ground black pepper to taste

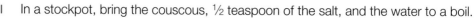

1   In a stockpot, bring the couscous, ½ teaspoon of the salt, and the water to a boil.

2   Turn the heat down to low. Cover and cook for 8 minutes, or until most of the water is absorbed.

3   When the couscous is cooked, drain it in a colander and rinse it with cool water. Set it aside.

4   Pour the lemon juice into a large bowl. Drizzle in the olive oil and whisk, adding the scallions and the remaining ½ teaspoon of salt.

5   Just before serving, add the arugula, tomatoes, feta cheese, and parsley to the couscous. Toss with the olive oil–lemon juice dressing. Season with pepper and serve.

FRESH TOMATOES
FROM THE FARMERS'
MARKET MAKE
THE DIFFERENCE IN
OUR ISRAELI
COUSCOUS SALAD

BROCCOLI RABE WITH GARLIC AND PINE NUTS

Though olive oil, garlic, and pine nuts usually please even the most dyed-in-the-wool herbi-phobe, the slightly bitter taste of broccoli rabe may scare off vegetable rookies. If you're cooking for the iceberg lettuce set, you can try this recipe with regular broccoli, and it will be just as tasty. • *Yield: 4 to 6 servings*

2 teaspoons salt
1 bunch broccoli rabe (about 1 pound),
1 inch of hard stems removed from the bottom
½ cup pine nuts
2 tablespoons olive oil
1 clove garlic, minced
2 lemon wedges
freshly ground black pepper to taste

1   Bring a pot of water to a boil. Add the salt. Add the broccoli rabe and cook for 3 to 4 minutes, until the broccoli is bright green. Remove it and rinse under cold water. Pat it dry and cut it into 1-inch-long pieces.

2   Meanwhile, toast the pine nuts in a skillet (no oil is necessary) over medium heat until they are light brown, about 4 minutes, turning often. Remove and set them aside.

3   Heat the oil in the skillet over medium heat. Add the garlic and cook for 1 minute.

4   Add the broccoli rabe, and sauté for 3 to 4 minutes.

5   Remove the broccoli and garlic from the heat and toss with the pine nuts. Squeeze the lemon wedges over the mixture. Add pepper to taste.

ITALIAN STRAWBERRY TART

This tart was inspired by a plum tart often cooked by the mother of Lisa's college roommate. Due to Lisa's reckless dissemination of that recipe (which caused an overpopulation of plum tarts up and down the eastern seaboard), her recipe-exchange privileges with said mother have been revoked. ▪ *Yield: 6 to 8 servings*

1½ cups flour

1½ teaspoons baking powder

¼ teaspoon salt

1 teaspoon cinnamon

6 tablespoons unsalted butter, softened

¾ cup sugar

2 eggs

2 tablespoons whole milk

1 pint strawberries, hulled and cut in half,
plus additional whole strawberries for garnish (optional)

fresh whipped cream (optional)

1   Preheat the oven to 350 degrees. Lightly grease a spring-form pan.

2   Mix together the flour, baking powder, salt, and cinnamon in a bowl.

3   In a separate bowl, beat the butter and the sugar. Add the eggs and milk. Add the dry ingredients to the egg mixture and stir by hand until just moistened. Do not overmix.

4   Spread the mixture into the bottom of the prepared pan. Press strawberry halves deeply into the dough in a circular pattern of 2 or 3 rings. Bake for 30 to 35 minutes, until a toothpick inserted in the center comes out clean. Serve warm with whipped cream and strawberries, if desired.

MEDITERRANEAN

MINI-ME MAC AND CHEESE

comfort

MENU

MINI-ME MAC AND CHEESE

OOOH BABY, IT'S
CHILI OUTSIDE!

BATTER-FRIED CHICKEN BITES

BEATEN-TO-WITHIN-
AN-INCH-OF-ITS-LIFE
SWEET POTATOES

PENNY'S BROCCOLI
CASSEROLE

CINNAMON RAISIN
BREAD PUDDIN'

stealing home

WE RAID MOM'S RECIPES IN SEARCH OF COZY COOKING

**COMFORT FOOD
NIGHT TAKES SHAPE
OVER E-MAIL:**

becky: i had a peanut butter and jelly sandwich for lunch and it instantly brought me back to second grade.

sharon: yum. i have such a craving for my mom's mashed potatoes.

cynthia: let's do a cooking club where all the food reminds us of childhood!

lucia: i used to eat paste when i was a child. does that count?

lisa: mmmm, mom-made mashed potatoes, mac and cheese, chicken pot pie . . .

becky: we could call it "six ways to get more starch in your diet."

katherine: or "food you can gum."

cynthia: enough, you two, or you'll get sent to your rooms.

The idea of doing comfort food as a theme came during a particularly depressing three-month stretch of winter. It was after New Year's but before spring-break season and there were no national holidays on the horizon (Presidents' Day was but a distant memory). The weather was miserable, so we figured we all needed a little comforting. And what better way to get it than with a little food nostalgia?

After the idea first came up, we tried to figure out exactly what comfort food was. Lisa claimed that it was derived from the Latin *comfortius foodius* and dated back hundreds of years. Becky maintained that its roots were firmly wedged in the meat-and-potatoes Midwest, while Katherine swore that the South birthed the concept of eating as an antidote to illness (or anything else, for that matter). Sharon believed that any Mom-made dishes qualified as comfort food; and Cynthia said, "If it makes you unbutton your pants, it's comfort food." Since the origins were so hazy, we decided to focus not on where it came from but why we loved it. It was warm, it was filling, one whiff reminded us of childhood, and it just oozed with home. Which is where we found the inspiration for many of these recipes.

Of course, the first time we attempted comfort food night, it really did end up as Six Ways to Get More Starch in Your Diet and yes, you could have eaten most of it without any teeth. It was so belly-expanding that it brought the idea of spa food night (see page 50) into being. As a result, the next time we held a comfort food night, we added veggies to the menu (even if they are covered with cheese, they're still greens, right?).

But while comfort foods can be on the heavy side, we all agreed that we liked feeling full and warm and sleepy after dinner. By far the most comforting thing about this Cooking Club meeting was that all our moms' recipes made Cooking Club feel like home, and the members like family.

COMFORT

MINI-ME MAC AND CHEESE

When word got out that a Cooking Club member was going to make mac and cheese, no fewer than four aunts, three mothers, and two friends offered up their special recipes for this wondrous dish. Of course, both friends' recipes included the word *Kraft,* but the four aunts' and three mothers' recipes were legit. We tossed them all in a pot and picked out our favorite parts of each to create this big dish of noodles, butter, and cheese. While the temptation to bury our heads in a pot of ooey-gooey goodness was strong, we decided to use six ramekins and serve them as appetizers, leaving room for all the other comforts that awaited us. • *Yield: 6 servings*

1 to 2 slices day-old bread
(enough to make ¼ cup breadcrumbs)
½ tablespoon olive oil
¼ cup Parmesan cheese
2½ cups uncooked macaroni
3 tablespoons butter
¼ cup flour
2 cups milk

1½ teaspoons dried mustard
¼ teaspoon cayenne pepper
1 teaspoon garlic powder
2 teaspoons Worcestershire sauce
¼ teaspoon salt
¼ teaspoon freshly ground
black pepper
3 cups sharp Cheddar cheese, grated

1   To prepare the breadcrumbs, cut the bread into cubes. In a food processor or blender, chop the bread until ground. On a baking sheet, spread out the crumbs and broil until toasted, about 3 minutes. In a bowl, toss the breadcrumbs with the olive oil and Parmesan cheese and set aside.

2   To prepare the pasta, in a large pot bring 8 cups of water to a boil. Add the pasta and cook until tender, about 7 minutes. Drain and set aside.

3   In a saucepan, melt the butter over low heat. Add the flour and whisk until blended. Add the milk. Bring to a boil, continually whisking so that the mixture doesn't stick to the pan. Add the mustard, cayenne pepper, garlic powder, Worcestershire sauce, salt, and black pepper. Simmer the sauce until it is thickened, about 2 minutes. Add 2½ cups of the Cheddar cheese. Stir until melted. Preheat the oven to broil.

4   Combine the pasta and cheese sauce in a bowl. Stir until the pasta is well coated. Spoon the mixture evenly into 6 small ramekins. Cover each top with some of the remaining Cheddar cheese and then sprinkle the breadcrumb mixture over each ramekin. Place the ramekins in a shallow baking dish and broil in the oven until the crumbs brown, about 1 to 2 minutes.

OOOH BABY, IT'S CHILI OUTSIDE!

Everybody had so many different ideas about what to put in the chili that we almost had an All Chili All the Time Cooking Club. That, of course, would have been, um, socially irresponsible. So we settled on this great basic recipe. Some like it hot (and be warned, this dish has some bite), but if you fear the fire, nix the chopped chilies. We set out bowls of shredded cheese, sour cream, and chives to garnish the chili. Or you could really go back to your roots and add a slice of American cheese on top with crumbled-up saltines over it (just the way our dads do it).
▪ *Yield: 4 to 6 servings*

2 pounds ground beef
¾ cup chopped onions
2 cloves garlic, minced
2 10½-ounce cans tomato soup
1 12-ounce bottle dark beer
1 15-ounce can diced tomatoes
2 tablespoons chili powder
1 teaspoon ground cumin
1 4-ounce can chopped chilies, drained
½ teaspoon salt
½ teaspoon pepper
1 16-ounce can kidney beans, undrained
1 16-ounce can pinto beans, undrained

1   In a large pot, brown the beef, onions, and garlic for 9 minutes.
2   Drain off the fat and stir in the remaining ingredients.
3   Cook for 1 hour over medium heat, stirring occasionally. Serve in individual bowls and top with desired garnishes.

BATTER-FRIED CHICKEN BITES

When Becky's husband, Steve, found out the Cooking Club theme of the month was comfort food, he lobbied hard to have it at their apartment—as a rule, the hosting member's husband/live-in boyfriend/roommate can attend since, well, he lives there. He also coerced Becky to make his mom's fried chicken. Bonnie, Becky's mom-in-law, is a high school home-economics teacher, so pretty much anything that comes out of her kitchen is amazing (ah, the added pressure for a new wife). When she sent along her recipe to Becky, she included this artery-clogging comment: "Growing up, Steven loved the chicken, but it was the fried dough I would make after dinner that was the real hit—just drop small spoonfuls of the leftover batter into the hot oil and fry until brown." You can serve the chicken with homemade honey mustard or barbecue sauce, or do what we did: Swipe a bunch of McDonald's Chicken McNugget sauces and pass it off to your guests as a kitschy appetizer. ▪ *Yield: 4 to 6 servings*

½ cup water

1 egg, beaten

2½ tablespoons sesame seeds

¾ cup flour

¼ teaspoon salt

½ teaspoon garlic powder

¼ teaspoon onion salt

dash of freshly ground black pepper

vegetable oil for frying

3 boneless, skinless chicken breasts,
cut into ½-inch-by-1-inch pieces

COMFORT

1   Preheat the oven to 275 degrees.

2   In a bowl, combine the first 8 ingredients to make the batter.

3   In a saucepan, heat 3 inches of oil (about 4 cups, depending on the size of the pan) on high.

4   Coat the chicken pieces with batter, then drop in the oil and submerge. Deep-fry for about 4 minutes, until golden brown, turning once.

5   Remove the chicken from the pan and set the pieces on a brown paper bag (it absorbs the grease better than paper towels—think Kentucky Fried Chicken). After draining, place the chicken on an ovenproof plate and set it in the oven to keep it warm and crisp until ready to serve.

BEATEN-TO-WITHIN-AN-INCH-OF-ITS-LIFE SWEET POTATOES

Five out of the six CC members remember eating marshmallow-topped sweet potatoes every Thanksgiving. We tried to grow up (just a little bit) and substituted honey and a little liquor instead. Top this with spicy pecans for an added kick and save the marshmallows for those Rice Krispies Treats you were going to make. • *Yield: 4 to 6 servings*

FOR THE SPICED PECANS:

8 tablespoons (1 stick) unsalted butter

½ cup light brown sugar

¼ teaspoon cayenne pepper

1 teaspoon coriander

2 cups chopped pecans

FOR THE POTATOES:

3 pounds sweet potatoes, peeled and cut into ½-inch pieces

6 tablespoons unsalted butter

1 tablespoon dark rum

⅓ cup light brown sugar, firmly packed

3 tablespoons honey

2 teaspoons grated fresh ginger

1 Preheat the oven to 350 degrees.

2 To prepare the pecans, melt the butter in a small bowl in the microwave. Add the brown sugar, cayenne pepper, and coriander. Stir well, and then add the nuts, coating them thoroughly. Spread the mixture on a baking sheet. Bake for 5 to 10 minutes, stirring occasionally. Allow to cool completely.

3 To prepare the potatoes, bring them to a boil in a large pot of salted water. Cook until tender, about 30 minutes. Drain the potatoes and place them in a large bowl.

4 Add the butter and dark rum and beat with an electric hand mixer until the potatoes are creamy. Stir in the brown sugar, honey, and ginger. Sprinkle pecans on top of each serving.

THE COOKING CLUB COOKBOOK

PENNY'S BROCCOLI CASSEROLE

Becky's aunt-in-law, Penny, served a version of this dish at her backyard wedding reception in 1985, so if this isn't a good-karma recipe, we don't know what is. They made two gallons of this delish dish; we suggest you stick to this quantity. • *Yield: 4 to 6 servings*

2 tablespoons unsalted butter

½ cup chopped onions

1 clove garlic, chopped

½ cup chopped celery

3 cups fresh broccoli, trimmed and chopped

2 cups cooked brown rice

1 10-ounce can condensed cream of chicken soup

½ cup milk

1 5-ounce can water chestnuts, drained and sliced

3 cups sharp Cheddar cheese, grated

1   Preheat the oven to 350 degrees.

2   Melt the butter in a 3-quart casserole dish.

3   Add the onions, garlic, and celery and microwave on high for 3 minutes, stirring halfway through. Add the broccoli and cook in the microwave on high for 4 minutes.

4   Stir in the cooked rice, soup, milk, water chestnuts, and 2½ cups of the cheese. Sprinkle the remaining ½ cup of cheese on top. Bake for 40 minutes, or until golden and bubbly.

COMFORT

CINNAMON RAISIN BREAD PUDDIN'

This recipe is as easy as, well, pudding. While perfect on its own, we've been known to add melted chocolate to satisfy certain members' addictions. • *Yield: 6 servings*

8 slices cinnamon raisin bread
2 eggs
¼ cup sugar
2 teaspoons vanilla
¼ teaspoon salt
2 cups milk
2 tablespoons unsalted butter
1 apple, peeled, cored, and thinly sliced
cinnamon-sugar topping
(mix 1 teaspoon cinnamon with ¼ cup sugar)

1   Preheat the oven to 350 degrees. Grease a loaf pan and set it aside. Cut the bread into 1-inch cubes and set aside.

2   In a large bowl, beat the eggs and sugar. Add the vanilla and salt and mix thoroughly. Meanwhile, in a saucepan heat the milk and butter over low heat until the butter is melted (do not let it boil). Add the hot milk mixture slowly to the egg mixture while whisking constantly. Set it aside.

3   Place half of the bread in the prepared pan. Layer the apple slices over the bread, then sprinkle with half of the cinnamon sugar. Layer the rest of the bread on top, pour the egg-milk mixture over it, and then sprinkle with the remaining cinnamon sugar.

4   Allow to stand for 5 minutes. Set the loaf pan in a larger baking dish, and add hot water to fill the baking dish halfway. Bake about 55 minutes. Check the pudding with a toothpick. If it comes out clean, it's done. It should be moist, not dry or runny. Serve warm with Cool Whip or ice cream.

COMFORT

SEARED SCALLOP SALAD
WITH HONEY-LIME VINAIGRETTE

spa

MENU

SEARED SCALLOP SALAD WITH
HONEY-LIME VINAIGRETTE

CUCUMBER GAZPACHO

GINGERED CARROTS

PORTOBELLO MUSHROOM AND
TOMATO TOWERS

LOW-FAT ZUCCHINI BREAD

APPLESAUCE CAKE
WITH LEMON GLAZE

spa go

CUTTING CALORIES FOR VANITY AND GOOD HEALTH, IN THAT ORDER

SPA NIGHT TAKES SHAPE OVER E-MAIL:

cynthia: ah, memorial day. nothing says first weekend of summer like the inevitable full-body waxing session. i can't wait.

katherine: yeah, that and getting reacquainted with our bikinis. lovely.

sharon: i want to go to a spa and be fed healthy meals. can cooking club go on a vacation?

lucia: are you paying?

becky: why don't we do our own little spa night?

lisa: don't you feel like tankinis totally cover up the wrong part? i mean, isn't it the bottom half that wants a bit of camouflage?

katherine: what does that have to do with spa night?

becky: everything.

In the wake of comfort food night, we wondered if CC was starting to stick to our ribs. Suddenly our skirts seemed snug and our pants felt tight. We worried that if we had more than one dinner where creamed corn counted as acceptable fare, we'd devolve into the Bring Your Own Stouffer's Pizza (Sweatsuit Attire Encouraged) Club. Like it or not, it was time to streamline CC's waistline.

Becky, the inventor of comfort food night and the loudest member rallying for beef, was, surprisingly, the first to propose a spa theme. With her Chicago wedding quickly approaching, she wanted to be able to fit into her dress—and have room for cake. Since both savings and scheduling made a research expedition to the Canyon Ranch Spa entirely out of the question, we decided to improvise. We vowed to log in some time at the gym by taking classes like boxing or Bikram yoga. Becky promised us a Sunday night reward in the form of seaweed and clay masks for every CC skin type, courtesy of her office beauty supply closet. And Sharon, who never misses a chance to cut calories, would oversee the menu. (Sharon's consistent attention to reduced-fat content is probably the only reason why we can still zip up our jeans, and why she works at *Spa Finder* magazine).

When we thought of spa food, the first thing that came to mind was dollhouse-sized portions of soy cake or bean-curd pizza. We feared we'd leave hungry after an entrée of bean sprouts or because the food was too bland. (Case in point: One of Sharon's first attempts at applesauce cake was such a flop that she was temporarily banned from dessert duty.) So the goal for Spa Go became to make dishes that were flavorful but didn't leave us in a post-Thanksgiving-style food coma.

We broke out the eucalyptus oils and juniper berry candles for a spa meal that was both filling and well balanced. Cynthia's Seared Scallop Salad with Honey-Lime Vinaigrette satisfied her designer's urge to make a beautifully arranged dish. It looked so pretty, the rest of us almost felt bad eating it—almost. Katherine's Cucumber Gazpacho was creamy and delicious; the hardest part about making it was waiting for it to cool. Lucia learned the delicate art of stacking foods for her Portobello Mushroom and Tomato Towers. Becky's Gingered Carrots really packed a punch, and Lisa's Low-Fat Zucchini Bread made with skim milk and applesauce proved that making substitutions for butter and oil can actually work when done correctly. But no spa meal would be complete without dessert, and Sharon's Applesauce Cake with Lemon Glaze was the perfect ending. The best part was that we could grab seconds without any pangs of guilt.

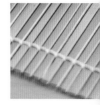

OUR UNDERRATED VEGGIE AWARD GOES TO THE HOMELY BUT TASTY JICAMA (THE POTATOLIKE ROOT SHARON'S DICING)

SEARED SCALLOP SALAD
WITH HONEY-LIME VINAIGRETTE

Scallops are the perfect spa food since they are low in fat and have only one hundred calories in a three-ounce serving. They are available year-round and come in three different varieties— sea, bay, and calico. We used sea scallops since they are the biggest and the meatiest—our Sunday night appetite wouldn't stand for anything less. Feel free to be creative with your salad: We added orange peppers and jicama to ours to give it color and crunch. • *Yield: 6 servings*

FOR THE DRESSING:
juice from 2 limes (⅓ cup)

5 teaspoons honey

1 tablespoon vinegar

⅛ teaspoon salt

1 tablespoon chopped chives, plus extra for garnish

FOR THE SCALLOPS:
2 pounds sea scallops

mixed greens (we used pea shoots, endive, and mesclun;
other suggestions: watercress, radicchio, and arugula)

assortment of chopped vegetables (we used
orange peppers and jicama; other suggestions:
hearts of palm, celery, and red peppers)

1   To make the dressing, in a bowl whisk together the lime juice, honey, vinegar, salt, and chives and stir.

2   Preheat a large nonstick skillet over medium-high heat.

3   Sear the scallops in the preheated skillet for 2 to 3 minutes on each side, until they become golden brown.

4   Remove the scallops from the pan and place them in a bowl. Coat the scallops with the honey-lime dressing.

5   Arrange a salad of mixed greens and an assortment of chopped vegetables on 6 serving plates. Drizzle the rest of the honey-lime dressing over the salads, then divide the scallops evenly among the plates of greens. Garnish with extra chives.

SPA

CUCUMBER GAZPACHO

Because most of us don't have dishwashers, a recipe that requires the use of a hard-to-wash appliance had better be good. When Katherine's family friend Mrs. Cox mentioned this cucumber soup for our spa night, we knew it was blender-worthy. Since this dish is easy to make and takes four hours to cool, Katherine had extra time to spend hand-washing the blender accoutrements. ▪ *Yield: 6 servings*

2 cups chicken or vegetable stock

2 medium cucumbers, peeled, seeded,
and cut into large pieces

2 cups plain nonfat yogurt

1 tablespoon vinegar

1 small clove garlic

salt and freshly ground black pepper to taste

assortment of vegetables (such as tomatoes, cucumbers,
green peppers, or black olives), chopped

1   Using a blender, combine all of the ingredients except the assorted chopped vegetables. (Depending on the size of your blender, you may need to make it in 2 batches.)

2   Cover and chill for at least 4 hours.

3   This dish is preferably made the day before and will keep up to a week in the refrigerator. Add assorted chopped veggies to the soup before serving.

GINGERED CARROTS

We couldn't have a spa chapter and not include at least one recipe containing ginger. Besides adding a great flavor, ginger is believed to have many healing properties. This dish is a colorful addition to any meal, an important feature since we believe that our food not only has to taste great but also should match our outfits. ▪ *Yield: 4 to 6 servings*

1 1-pound bag cleaned baby carrots
1 teaspoon ground ginger
¾ cup orange juice
1 tablespoon dark brown sugar
½ teaspoon sugar
1 teaspoon cornstarch
salt and freshly ground black pepper to taste

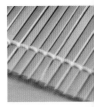

1 Cook the carrots in boiling water for 10 minutes or until the carrots are slightly tender, then drain them.

2 Mix the ginger, orange juice, both sugars, and cornstarch in a bowl.

3 Place the cooked carrots and the ginger mixture in a saucepan and cook over medium heat, stirring occasionally, until the mixture thickens, forming a glaze over the carrots. Add salt and pepper before serving.

PORTOBELLO MUSHROOM
AND TOMATO TOWERS

Portobello mushrooms by nature have no fat, but they do have a fabulous flavor and a meaty texture. Grilled, broiled, or roasted, portobello mushrooms can stand in for anything, from T-bones to burgers. We paired them with tomatoes and soaked them in a balsamic vinegar–based marinade. All we have left to say is "Yum." ▪ *Yield: 6 servings*

FOR THE BALSAMIC DRESSING:

6 tablespoons balsamic vinegar

4 teaspoons mustard

4 teaspoons honey

1 teaspoon garlic powder

¼ teaspoon salt

FOR THE TOWERS:

12 portobello mushroom caps

3 large tomatoes

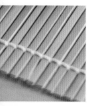

1   Preheat the oven to broil.

2   Mix the dressing ingredients in a bowl and soak the portobello mushroom caps in the dressing for 1 hour.

3   Broil the portobello mushrooms round side up in a broiler pan for 2 to 3 minutes. Turn the mushrooms and cook with the gill side up for 4 to 5 minutes.

4   Slice each tomato into 6 pieces, about ½ inch thick.

5   Place a tomato slice on a plate and stack a portobello mushroom cap on top of it. Place another tomato slice on top of that, then the second portobello mushroom, then top with the last piece of tomato. Do the same on 5 more plates, then pour the rest of the dressing over all, allowing some to fall over the sides of each tower.

LOW-FAT ZUCCHINI BREAD

Look for small zucchinis to use for this dish, since the smaller the squash, the sweeter the flavor. To add even more nutrition to spa night, we added sunflower seeds, which are cholesterol-free and a good source of protein and vitamin E. • *Yield: 1 loaf*

3 cups flour

1 tablespoon baking powder

½ teaspoon baking soda

1 teaspoon salt

2 teaspoons cinnamon

1 teaspoon nutmeg

½ cup skim milk

½ teaspoon vanilla

1 egg white, beaten to a stiff peak

¾ cup applesauce

1 cup sugar

2 small zucchinis, grated (2 cups)

cooking spray

⅓ cup unsalted sunflower seeds

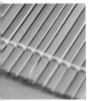

1   Preheat the oven to 350 degrees.

2   In a large bowl, combine the flour, baking powder, baking soda, salt, cinnamon, and nutmeg.

3   In another bowl, combine the milk, vanilla, egg white, applesauce, sugar, and zucchini.

4   Add the wet ingredients to the dry and stir until blended, but do not overmix.

5   Pour the batter into a 9-by-5-inch pan, lightly greased with nonfat cooking spray. Add the sunflower seeds to the top of the loaf and bake for 50 to 60 minutes, until a toothpick inserted in the center comes out clean.

APPLESAUCE CAKE WITH LEMON GLAZE

Fruit salad is fine for breakfast, but it's a far cry from cake. To avoid spa-dessert disappointment, we substituted applesauce for the oil to create this indulgent but fat-free finale to our meal.

FOR THE CAKE:

cooking spray

1½ cups applesauce

1 cup sugar

2 eggs (egg substitute can be used instead)

1½ teaspoons baking soda

2 cups flour

FOR THE LEMON GLAZE:

¾ cup sugar

¼ cup fresh lemon juice (about 1 lemon)

1   Preheat the oven to 350 degrees.

2   Lightly grease a cake pan with cooking spray.

3   Put the applesauce, sugar, and eggs in a bowl and mix. Add the baking soda, and gradually stir in the flour.

4   Pour into a cake pan and bake for 40 minutes or until a toothpick inserted in the center comes out clean.

5   While the cake is baking, mix the sugar and lemon juice in a bowl to make a glaze.

6   When the cake is done, use a fork to poke holes in it while it is still hot from the oven. Spoon the glaze over the top and let it cool.

SPA

sexy

MENU

BAKED PESTO OYSTERS
ON THE HALF-SHELL

APHRODISIAC SALAD

SLICED FLANK STEAK WITH
PAPAYA-KIWI MARINADE

WILD GINGER RICE

ASPARAGUS WITH CHARDONNAY-
CAVIAR CREAM SAUCE

ALL-ABOUT-THE-CHOCOLATE CAKE
WITH RASPBERRY COULIS

sex and the kitchen

SUNDAY NIGHT IS SUDDENLY HOT AND STEAMY

SEXY NIGHT TAKES SHAPE OVER E-MAIL:

sharon: i'm coming to our next meeting only if we can watch *sex and the city* afterward. i can't miss it. i'm addicted.

becky: brilliant. i was waiting for someone else to suggest it.

lisa: though last week the show kind of annoyed me—how can carrie afford to buy manolo blahnik stilettos and drink twelve-dollar cosmopolitans every night on a journalist's salary?

katherine: maybe she skips the food and just drinks cosmos for dinner.

lucia: maybe carrie should stop being so sexy and join a cooking club.

cynthia: what?! cooking club *is* sexy. well, at least sexier than my old crafts club.

becky: crafts club? oh, cynthia . . .

First, a disclaimer: We are fully aware that this theme entails six women cooking sexy food for each other. Almost every male who heard about our sexy foods night responded with an "Oh, really?" as slimy as roasted eggplant. Note that we are not *that* kind of club. The purpose of our sexy foods night was to create an utterly sophisticated, sinfully sensual meal, using recipes our moms most likely *never* used to make (at least not for us). Plus, we figured it couldn't hurt for all of us to learn how to whip up an aphrodisiac appetizer or a seduce-me steak, because such a skill just might be needed in a non–Cooking Club situation.

Second, we realize you may be wondering what sexy foods are. Good question. It's hard to get six dinner courses out of strawberries, whipped cream, and licorice whips. So we kept the category broad, and so should you. For instance, if oysters remind you of summers at the lake house with Grandpa Buster, then you should substitute any food that *you* associate with sexiness. But for the most part, we think we've found some pretty universal crowd pleasers. For example, most people find that eating chocolate gives them an extremely pleasant sensation similar to, er, another extremely pleasant physical sensation. That's why for our dinner, Becky, who was bringing dessert, didn't mess around—her flourless chocolate cake is all about the chocolate. (In fact, it's actually called All-About-the-Chocolate Cake.)

To get some ideas for our dinner, Katherine did an Internet search for edible aphrodisiacs, and found that the infamous oyster came up as the food most widely believed to have stimulating powers, but so did various nuts and vegetables, as well as many exotic fruits and spices. (She actually found several other things on the Internet under the topic "sexy foods," the most intriguing of which were instructions for a Master/Slave Seduction Crab Legs dinner. Surely tasty, but not quite right for our cooking club.)

But we wanted our sexy dinner to go beyond just aphrodisiac ingredients. We were all well versed in the language of women's magazines, and therefore aware of the following theorem: The sexiest kind of woman is a confident woman. So we extrapolated: The sexiest kind of food is a confident food. The boldest food we could think of was, of course, red meat. Lucia's delicious Sliced Flank Steak with Papaya-Kiwi Marinade was a hit, and Cynthia, not to be outdone, sexed up the meal with her own luscious dish—what became known as Aphrodisiac Salad. The vinaigrette she made calls for champagne, so she brought the rest of the bottle over for us to drink with the appetizers. In fact, we recommend having whoever is on salad duty bring ingredients to make sexy drinks as well, the options for which are endless, from watermelon champagne to Belvedere martinis to cosmopolitans. The real fun of this dinner is that even if you're in sweatpants, the food will make you feel like you're decked out in snakeskin and slingbacks.

BAKED PESTO OYSTERS ON THE HALF-SHELL

Legend has it that Casanova ate seventy raw oysters a day, often in the bathtub. Whether it's true that oysters are what made him so popular with the ladies, they do contain large amounts of zinc, which supposedly helps to increase sexual desire in both men and women. We'll let you test that theory yourselves. But we can tell you that these oysters, baked with pesto on top (pine nuts are also thought to be an aphrodisiac), make a deliciously decadent appetizer. Note that blistered fingers are *not* sexy; buy the oysters shucked, no more than a few hours before preparation. • *Yield: 6 servings*

2 cups coarse salt

1¼ cups fresh basil

½ cup pine nuts, toasted
(see directions for pan-toasting on page 34)

3 tablespoons water

2 teaspoons fresh lemon juice

2 large cloves garlic, chopped

6 tablespoons olive oil

½ teaspoon salt

½ teaspoon freshly ground black pepper

½ cup breadcrumbs

¼ cup Parmesan cheese, freshly grated

2 dozen fresh oysters on the half-shell, drained of juice

1   Cover the bottom of a baking dish with the salt and place it in a 400-degree oven for 30 minutes.

2   To prepare the pesto, combine the basil, pine nuts, water, lemon juice, and garlic in a food processor. Blend well, until finely chopped. Add the olive oil, salt, and pepper and blend until the mixture is smooth.

3   Combine the breadcrumbs and cheese and set aside.

4   Leaving the oysters in the half-shell, place the shells on the salt, and return the pan to the oven for 5 minutes.

5   Remove the pan from the oven and spoon the pesto sauce over each oyster, then generously sprinkle with the breadcrumb-and-cheese mixture.

6   Continue cooking until lightly browned, about 5 minutes. Place 4 oysters on each plate and serve immediately.

DOES SHE WANT
HIM ONLY FOR HIS
BAKED GOODS?
A FEISTY BECKY
MAKES HER MOVE

APHRODISIAC SALAD

We loved this salad for our dinner, and highly recommend it for a romantic dinner for two. It's little work for a lot of pleasure. If the combination of fresh figs, walnuts, and crumbled blue cheese doesn't get your juices flowing, we don't know what will. Maybe the champagne vinaigrette dribbling off your dinner companion's chin will do the trick. ▪ *Yield: 4 to 6 servings*

FOR THE SALAD:
6 cups mixed salad greens
¾ cup fresh figs, quartered
½ cup walnuts, halved
**½ cup crumbled Stilton cheese
(or any blue cheese if not available)**

FOR THE CHAMPAGNE VINAIGRETTE:
1 tablespoon champagne vinegar
1 tablespoon champagne (optional)
3 tablespoons bland oil, such as sunflower
1 tablespoon extra-virgin olive oil
Salt and freshly ground black pepper to taste

1   Combine the salad ingredients.
2   For the dressing, whisk the champagne vinegar and champagne (if using) together in a small bowl. Slowly whisk in the 3 tablespoons of bland oil until the mixture is thickened, then whisk in the olive oil. Add salt and pepper to taste.
3   Drizzle the dressing over the salad right before serving.

SLICED FLANK STEAK WITH PAPAYA-KIWI MARINADE

The longer you marinate your flank steak, the more tender and flavorful the end result will be. (Think of it as culinary foreplay.) So whoever brings this dish should make the marinade the night before or that morning so that the meat will have at least five hours to absorb the flavors of these fresh exotic fruits. ▪ *Yield: 4 to 6 servings*

1 large ripe papaya, peeled and sliced

3 kiwis, peeled and sliced

2 tablespoons balsamic vinegar

1 tablespoon light brown sugar

2 large shallots, finely chopped

2 tablespoons olive oil

½ tablespoon honey

2 tablespoons fresh lemon juice

2 tablespoons chopped parsley

1 tablespoon minced garlic

1 teaspoon salt

2 teaspoons freshly ground black pepper

1 2-pound flank steak, trimmed

1   Put the papaya and kiwis in a food processor and pulse until just finely chopped but not pureed.

2   Combine the papaya-kiwi mixture, vinegar, and sugar in a saucepan and cook over medium heat for about 5 minutes, stirring often. Remove from the heat and let it cool. Reserve ½ cup.

3   Combine the shallots, olive oil, honey, lemon juice, parsley, garlic, salt, and pepper in a bowl. Add the cooled fruit mixture and mix.

4   Place the steak in a glass dish. Cover it with the mixture and marinate, covered, up to 24 hours in the refrigerator, turning the steak occasionally.

5   Preheat the broiler. Remove the steak from the marinade and broil to the desired doneness, about 4 minutes per side for medium-rare.

6   Thinly slice the steak across the grain on a diagonal. Drizzle the remaining ½ cup fruit mixture over the meat and serve.

WILD GINGER RICE

Lisa told us she once read that the Puritans would not allow ginger in their diets because it heats the blood, so she was eager to know if we felt any hotter after eating her gingery side dish. We did, but only because of the energy exerted in order to consume the whole delicious pot of it. ▪ *Yield: 4 to 6 servings*

2½ tablespoons salted butter
½ cup onion, finely chopped
1 tablespoon fresh ginger, grated
1½ cups converted white rice
1½ cups chicken broth
¾ cup slivered almonds
⅓ cup cilantro, coarsely chopped
⅓ cup celery, finely chopped
⅓ cup green pepper, finely chopped

1   Melt the butter in a large saucepan over medium heat. Add the onions and cook until soft, about 3 to 4 minutes. Stir in the ginger and cook for an additional 2 minutes.

2   Stir in the rice. Add the chicken broth and stir. Cover and cook for 20 minutes over low-medium heat.

3   Stir in the almonds, cilantro, celery, and green pepper, re-cover, and cook for 2 more minutes. Serve warm.

ASPARAGUS WITH CHARDONNAY-CAVIAR CREAM SAUCE

As far as aphrodisiacs go, you can't forget wine, as Sharon reminded us. Her asparagus topped with a Chardonnay cream sauce was ooh . . . la la. We sprinkled black caviar on top of the sauce—truly sexy people are always sprinkling caviar on top. • *Yield: 4 to 6 servings*

2 pounds asparagus, trimmed
1½ tablespoons unsalted butter
1½ tablespoons vegetable oil
3 large shallots, finely chopped
⅓ cup Chardonnay
2 teaspoons lemon zest
1½ cups heavy cream
1½ teaspoons dried chervil
2 ounces black caviar

1   Blanch the asparagus in a large pot of boiling salted water for 2 minutes. Transfer to a colander and rinse under cold running water to stop the cooking. Drain well and pat dry.
2   Heat the butter and oil in a saucepan over medium heat until the butter is melted. Add the shallots and cook until soft, about 5 minutes. Add the wine and lemon zest. Simmer for 3 minutes. Add the cream and chervil. Simmer for about 15 more minutes, until thick.
3   Pour the sauce over the asparagus. Sprinkle on the caviar and serve immediately.

SEXY

SEX POTS (AND PANS
BECKY (LEFT) POURS
IT ON FOR SEXY
FOOD NIGHT, AS
SHARON OVERSEES

ALL-ABOUT-THE-CHOCOLATE CAKE WITH RASPBERRY COULIS

By the time you get to dessert, you should definitely be feeling the love. And this pure decadence disguising itself in the form of a cake will put you right over the edge. It's flourless and cooked inside an outer pan of water, so the resulting cake is rich, thick, moist . . . I think you know where this is going. • *Yield: 6 to 8 servings*

FOR THE CAKE:

8 ounces good-quality
semisweet baking chocolate

8 tablespoons (1 stick)
unsalted butter

¼ cup sugar

4 eggs, separated

1 teaspoon vanilla

¼ teaspoon salt

1 tablespoon dark brown
sugar, firmly packed

FOR THE COULIS:

12 ounces fresh raspberries
(reserve ½ cup for garnish)

2 tablespoons sugar

rum or orange-flavor
liqueur (optional)

1 Preheat the oven to 350 degrees.

2 In a medium saucepan, melt the chocolate and the butter. Stir over low heat until smooth. Stir in the sugar until dissolved. Remove from the heat. Let the mixture cool slightly. Add the egg yolks one by one, mixing well after each addition. Stir in the vanilla. Set aside.

3 In a medium-size bowl, beat the egg whites with the salt until foamy. Add the brown sugar. Beat until soft peaks form. Fold the whites into the chocolate mixture.

4 Pour the batter into a buttered 9-inch cake pan. Set the pan inside a larger pan filled with boiling water about halfway up the sides of the cake pan. Place in the center of the oven and cook for approximately 30 minutes. Do not overcook. When a toothpick inserted in the center of the cake comes out clean, the cake is done. While the cake is cooling, prepare the coulis.

5 Puree the fruit and sugar in a food processor. Strain through a fine sieve. Stir in the liqueur, if desired.

6 Cover 6 individual dessert plates with coulis. Place a slice of warm cake on each plate and top with the reserved raspberries.

SEXY

GRILLED CORN AND POTATO SALAD

grill

MENU

SHRIMP ON THE BARBIE

GRILLED TUNA SALAD

MILE-HIGH BURGERS

VEGETABLE COZIES

GRILLED CORN AND POTATO SALAD

COCONUT ANGEL FOOD CAKE
WITH RUM-DRUNK
GRILLED PINEAPPLE

grills' night out

WE LIGHT OUR OWN FIRE

GRILL NIGHT TAKES SHAPE OVER E-MAIL:

becky: i vote for a menu that's more indigenous to our native american land.

lisa: is this a cry to rally around the midwest-is-best theme?

cynthia: you mean nouveau american? i love stacked food!

lucia: i thought stacked food was a new york city thing. you know, small tables, small plates, tall food.

becky: i mean, prepared the american way. c'mon, think summer. think beach, think girl scouts . . .

sharon: oooh, i love girl scout cookies! did you get a recipe for thin mints?

katherine: thin mints will not make us thin nor are they a mint. discuss.

cynthia: if you're suggesting that we hunt and kill our own food, i'm putting you on cc probation.

Summer in the city threatens to send CC members on hiatus from cooking (we can't stand the heat, so we definitely don't want to be in the kitchen). As a result, the summer months were always filled with everything stovetop-free: salads, chilled soups, and fruit smoothies. But since we're a cooking club eager to expand our culinary skills, we couldn't just ignore the most basic and primal of summer traditions: grilling!

In New York City, backyards equipped with Weber grills are in short supply. In fact, backyards are in short supply, as are any grassy knolls or open spaces. So our choices seemed limited: hanging out the window with a mini propane grill balanced delicately on a fire escape, or starting a campfire in Central Park. Both options would be followed immediately by some jail time, of course, but at least we would have had a freshly grilled ear of corn. Just when we were about to settle for roasting marshmallows over a gas-stove burner, Becky's savvy future mother-in-law provided her, and hence the Cooking Club, with the brilliant bridal-shower gift of an indoor grill. So it came to pass that CC met on a steamy July evening to christen the new gift and boldly declare, "If it's not nailed down, we're grilling it!"

Of course, grilling indoors is not without its problems. It took only one lone sizzling burger on the alleged "smokeless" grill to force a Cooking Club member to rip the smoke detector from the ceiling. (Note to fire warden: As soon as dinner was finished, said detector was reinstalled.)

But grilling turned out to be a bigger challenge than keeping the fire department from knocking down our door (not that we'd be opposed to having a band of strapping firemen over for dinner). Instead, we had to design six dishes around the method of cooking, not just what was put in them. Since we couldn't envision six completely charbroiled entrées, the one requirement for Grills' Night Out was that every dish had to include an ingredient that was actually grilled. A well-thought-out move, since it became evident that you can't grill a coconut angel food cake, although you *can* grill rum-basted pineapples to accompany it. Who knew?

After the success of our first grilling adventure, we decided that barbecuing definitely had to become an annual theme. And it did, but Becky's indoor grill eventually got shoved to the back of the cupboard. Instead, we exploited every parent, friend, and coworker who had any kind of outdoor cooking arena in a three-county radius. As it turned out, open spaces and grassy knolls really *do* make a difference when it comes to the joy of grilling.

GRILL

SHRIMP ON THE BARBIE

A very wise Cooking Club member once said, "You could pretty much wrap bacon around a wad of cotton balls and it would be delicious." Oh, how true that is. But even though we all need fiber in our diet, we kept the cotton balls in the medicine cabinet and tried wrapping the bacon around shrimp instead. The most challenging part of this recipe is the construction of the dish. After several jalapeños jumped to a fiery death and cheese oozed all over the grill, we finally found a way to secure all the ingredients in a snug little package. The trick is to keep the cheese slice long and very thin so that it can actually be wrapped around the shrimp and covered completely by the bacon. • *Yield: 4 to 6 servings*

1 cup olive oil

½ cup freshly squeezed lime juice

¼ cup Worcestershire sauce

3 tablespoons fresh tarragon, chopped

1 pound (about 20) precooked large peeled shrimp
(with tails on)

1 pound bacon

½ pound Monterey jack cheese,
sliced into thin 2-inch-long strips

3 jalapeño peppers, cored, seeded,
and sliced into small pieces

I   In a small bowl, combine the oil, lime juice, Worcestershire sauce, and tarragon. Soak the shrimp in this marinade, cover, and chill for 2 hours. After 1 hour, soak 20 to 25 short wooden skewers in a bowl of cold water.

2   Cut the bacon to allow each piece to wrap all the way around the shrimp, with a bit of overlap. (Half a slice is usually enough.)

3   Lay a piece of bacon flat on a working space. Place a cheese slice over it. Lay a shrimp in the middle with the tail hanging over the bacon, and top with a jalapeño piece. Pull one end of the bacon over the shrimp, and then the other. Pierce with a skewer, and be sure to stab the jalapeño to secure it.

4   Place the skewers on a preheated grill over medium heat. Rotate often (these little guys need to be looked after; leave them unattended and they will burn). Cook until all the bacon has been browned. Place on a platter and serve.

GRILLED TUNA SALAD

This is great as a main dish for mad cow–fearing members, or as a flavorful side salad. Be sure to watch the tuna on the grill. This recipe is for seared tuna, but you can cook it longer if you like. (It shouldn't be on more than five minutes for each side or it will start to get dry.) • *Yield: 4 to 6 servings*

FOR THE TUNA:
2 tablespoons olive oil, plus additional for grill
1 tablespoon paprika
1 tablespoon chili powder
3 cloves garlic, minced
2 teaspoons dried oregano
¼ cup freshly squeezed grapefruit juice
4 sushi-grade tuna steaks (6 to 8 ounces each)

FOR THE SALAD DRESSING:
6 tablespoons grapefruit juice
¼ cup olive oil
2 tablespoons red wine vinegar
1 tablespoon chopped fresh mint

12 cups romaine lettuce or various greens
2 grapefruits, peeled and sectioned,
membrane and pith removed, for garnish

GRILL

1   Combine 2 tablespoons of olive oil and the paprika, chili powder, garlic, and oregano in a food processor and mix until smooth. Add the grapefruit juice and blend well. Place the tuna in a baking dish and pour the marinade over it. Cover and refrigerate it for 2 hours.

2   Meanwhile, to make the salad dressing, in a small bowl whisk together the grapefruit juice, oil, vinegar, and mint, then refrigerate. (The dressing can be made up to 2 hours ahead.)

3   Brush the grill with olive oil. Preheat the grill to very hot, then cook the tuna until brown on both sides, about 1½ to 2 minutes per side.

4   Toss the greens with the dressing in a large bowl. Place 2 cups of greens on each plate. Cut the fish fillets into several slices and lay them on top of the individual salads. Serve garnished with several slices of grapefruit.

MILE-HIGH BURGERS

Burgers, in whatever form, are a prerequisite if you're grilling. This recipe is a great alternative to the old standby. It was such a hit that Katherine declared it "meatloaf on the grill." So toss your buns aside; this burger stands alone. • *Yield: 6 servings*

2 8-ounce cans tomato sauce
1 teaspoon dried thyme
1 teaspoon dried oregano
1 teaspoon dried rosemary
3 cloves garlic, minced
⅔ cup white wine
1 cup pitted green olives, sliced
2 pounds ground chuck
1 egg
2 teaspoons seasoned salt
¼ teaspoon freshly ground black pepper
6 slices mozzarella cheese
1 onion, thinly sliced
½ cup Parmesan cheese

I   In a saucepan, mix together the tomato sauce, thyme, oregano, rosemary, garlic, and wine and bring to a boil. Reduce the heat and stir in the olives. Cook for 5 minutes, then remove from the heat and set aside.

2   To prepare the burgers, mix the ground chuck with the egg, salt, and pepper. Form 6 patties, about 1½ inches thick.

3   Cook the burgers on a preheated grill (medium to high heat) until brown on one side, approximately 5 minutes. Flip, cook for about 2 minutes, then place a slice of mozzarella cheese on top. Add a spoonful of sauce, a couple of slices of onion, and then more sauce. Sprinkle with Parmesan cheese. Serve with warm garlic bread on the side if you desire. Keep the sauce at table for additional spooning.

Raisin
Walnut rolls
$1.25   3 for $2.00

Baggette
$2.00

CHALLACH
$3.50 /lg
$2.50 /sm

UNABLE TO FATHOM
A STARCHLESS MEAL,
LISA CONSIDERS
SNEAKING A SIDE OF
BREAD FOR BECKY'S
BUNLESS BURGERS

VEGETABLE COZIES

We've prepared vegetables a number of ways on the grill, but none keep the flavor as well as steaming them in individual aluminum-foil cozies. We originally tried to jazz up this dish with fancy dips and sauces, but when we got right down to it, nothing was better than some great spices on excellent summer veggies. We love using fresh herbs, but if you don't have any on hand, reduce the spice measurements by half and use dried herbs. • *Yield: 6 servings*

½ cup olive oil
½ teaspoon fresh chopped basil, or ¼ teaspoon dried
½ teaspoon fresh chopped tarragon, or ¼ teaspoon dried
1 teaspoon fresh chopped oregano, or ½ teaspoon dried
2 cloves garlic, minced
1 zucchini, sliced
1 red pepper, sliced
12 large mushrooms, halved
1½ cups pearl onions
18 asparagus, peeled and cut in half
½ cup Parmesan cheese
salt and freshly ground black pepper to taste

1   In a bowl, combine the oil, basil, tarragon, oregano, and garlic.

2   Divide the vegetables among 6 aluminum-foil sheets (each about 12 inches square). Drizzle 2 spoonfuls of the oil mixture over each package. Sprinkle with Parmesan cheese and season with salt and pepper.

3   Fold the aluminum foil up over the veggies and place on a preheated grill (medium to high heat) until tender, about 15 minutes.

GRILLED CORN AND POTATO SALAD

This potato salad is a great base if you want to add other veggies as well. We've tossed in green beans, cucumbers, and some really exotic vegetable that Cynthia found in Chinatown (we don't recommend that one, though). The mustard dressing can be made the day before, covered, and refrigerated. Allow the dressing to come to room temperature before serving.

▪ *Yield: 6 servings*

3 ears of corn in husks
1½ tablespoons mustard
3 tablespoons cider vinegar
½ cup olive oil
2 pounds small new potatoes
2 cups sugar snap peas
1 cup cherry tomatoes, halved
salt and freshly ground black pepper to taste

GRILL

1   To keep the corn husks from burning when placed on the grill, soak the corn in cold water for 30 minutes (set a plate on top of the ears to keep them submerged).

2   In a small bowl, combine the mustard and vinegar. Add the oil and whisk until blended. Set the dressing aside.

3   In a pot, cover the potatoes with salted water, bring to a boil, and simmer for about 30 minutes, until tender. Drain the potatoes and transfer them to a large bowl. Cut them into bite-size chunks.

4   Fill a bowl with cold water and ice. Set it aside. In a pot of boiling water, cook the snap peas for 1 minute, then transfer them with a slotted spoon to the ice-water bath. Drain and add the peas to the potatoes. Add the tomatoes.

5   Remove the corn from the water, drain it, and toss it on a preheated grill (medium to high heat), turning occasionally, for about 12 to 15 minutes, until the outer leaves are charred. Remove and let it stand for a couple of minutes to avoid burned fingers when you shuck it. Return the corn to the grill to brown it a little bit. (You want your guests to know that you didn't just grab the Jolly Green Giant out of the freezer, don't you?)

6   Cut the corn kernels off the cob with a serrated knife, add to the potato mixture, and toss with the desired amount of dressing and salt and pepper to taste.

OUR GRILL
NIGHT MOTTO
"IF IT'S NOT
NAILED DOWN
WE'RE GRILLI
IT." PINEAPPL
SKEWERS ARE
NO EXCEPTIO

COCONUT ANGEL FOOD CAKE WITH RUM-DRUNK GRILLED PINEAPPLE

The first time the Cooking Club made angel food cake (you know, not from a box), the flour wasn't sifted before it was added (which explains why it wasn't so angel light). The addition of coconut makes this cake richer than a traditional angel food cake. • *Yield: 6 servings*

FOR THE CAKEY-CAKE:

¾ cup flour (all-purpose)

8 fresh egg whites, brought to room temperature

1 tablespoon warm water

½ teaspoon salt

½ teaspoon cream of tartar

1 cup sugar

1 teaspoon almond extract

½ cup plus 2 tablespoons shredded coconut

FOR THE PINEAPPLE:

6 wooden skewers

¾ cup dark rum

¾ cup light brown sugar, firmly packed

2 teaspoons vanilla extract

½ teaspoon ground cinnamon

1 large pineapple, peeled, cored, and cut into 1-inch pieces

1   Preheat the oven to 350 degrees. Soak wooden skewers in water for 1 hour.

2   To prepare the cake, sift the flour twice into a small bowl. Set it aside. In a large bowl, beat the egg whites, water, salt, and cream of tartar with an electric mixer until soft peaks form. Gradually beat in the sugar and almond extract. Beat until stiff peaks form.

3   Sift the flour over the whites in 3 batches, folding it in gently after each addition. Fold in ½ cup of coconut.

4   Sprinkle the 2 tablespoons of coconut onto the bottom of a lightly greased nonstick bundt pan. Spoon the batter into the pan and bake the cake in the middle of the oven for 50 minutes or until a toothpick inserted into the center comes out clean.

5   Hang the cake in the pan upside down on the neck of a bottle and let it cool completely, about 2 hours. Release the cake with a sharp knife and turn it out, inverted, onto a cake plate, with the coconut on top. Cut it into the desired number of slices.

6   To prepare the pineapple, mix the first 4 ingredients together in a small bowl until the sugar dissolves.

7   Stack the pineapple pieces onto the skewers, then place the skewers on a preheated grill over medium heat and baste with the rum mixture.

8   Grill the pineapple until browned, turning to get all the sides coated and cooked, about 10 minutes. To serve, remove the pineapple from the skewers and pile it on top of the slices of angel food cake. Drizzle any remaining rum mixture over the cake.

BANANAS FOSTER WITH
PRALINED PECANS

mardi gras

MENU

OYSTERS ROCKEFELLER
SPINACH DIP

CREOLE CASSEROLE
WITH EGGPLANT,
SHRIMP, AND CRABMEAT

BEER BISCUITS

TURKEY SAUSAGE AND
CHICKEN GUMBO

OKRA AND TOMATOES

BANANAS FOSTER
WITH PRALINED
PECANS

low-fat tuesday
THE LIGHTER SIDE OF CREOLE CUISINE

MARDI GRAS NIGHT TAKES SHAPE OVER E-MAIL:

katherine: i need help! my craving for new orleans food has become so bad that last night i dreamed i was watching a musical performed by fried oysters.

sharon: then let's have a new orleans night. i don't know about fried oysters but i could make something equally decadent.

cynthia: sharon, you're the low-fat queen. think about what you're saying.

lisa: why do people in louisiana eat such rich food, anyway? it's not like they have to store up for a cold winter.

lucia: i think they need something to soak up the alcohol.

becky: ah, my kind of town.

During Mardi Gras (or Fat Tuesday) in New Orleans, indulgence is not only encouraged but sanctified. We liked the sound of that, and thought it would be the perfect theme for a Cooking Club dinner. But as we began to plan six authentic New Orleans–style dishes, we kept encountering one particular stumbling block—would we be able to stand up after eating them? The large quantities of butter that most of the recipes called for (not to mention rich ingredients such as crabmeat, oysters, and bacon drippings) gave us pause. After all, we weren't actually in New Orleans, where we would have a typical fat-burning day of Mardi Gras (catching beads and drinking beer) ahead of us to justify such a heavy meal. So we decided to create a dinner that preserved the unique flavors and flair of New Orleans cuisine, but without the copious cholesterol. And Katherine, who grew up in New Orleans, had the perfect recipe resource for just such a meal—her mom, a Southern woman who understands the equal merits of a sinful meal and a svelte physique.

What makes Creole cuisine such a great theme for a Cooking Club dinner is the wide range of cultural influences that make the food so flavorful. In fact, some say the food in New Orleans is the best in the world. (Take a guess which Cooking Club member made that claim and we'll send you a free bottle of Tabasco.) A typical gumbo recipe, for example, contains ingredients from Europe to the West Indies. The dish is said to have originated from one early French settler's desire to re-create his beloved bouillabaisse, but he had to replace the Mediterranean fish with whatever seafood he could find in the Gulf. And the word *gumbo* is actually the African word for okra, which is still used today in many gumbo recipes.

So you should feel free to incorporate ingredients from your own respective regions. Polish sausage, for example, could be used in our Turkey Sausage and Chicken Gumbo, or New England clams could be substituted in our Oysters Rockefeller Spinach Dip. Of course, you'll have to draw the line somewhere; cooks from California might be out of luck, as no self-respecting Creole dish should include a bean sprout, or, for that matter, any na-ture of soy product. (It's enough that we're replacing twelve tablespoons of butter with two of canola oil in our version of Creole Casserole with Eggplant, Shrimp, and Crabmeat.)

Low-Fat Tuesday night was a success—we were able to indulge our taste buds as well as stand up comfortably afterward. So put on a Harry Connick, Jr., album, find the cayenne pepper on your spice rack, get out your silver monogrammed mint julep cups (okay, maybe this one's a stretch), and have fun re-creating these somewhat lighter versions of authentic Creole dishes.

OYSTERS ROCKEFELLER SPINACH DIP

Oysters Rockefeller is a famous New Orleans recipe involving baked oysters on the half-shell, parsley or spinach topping, and, of course, butter. Sharon already had a great recipe for a low-fat hot spinach dip, but by adding oysters and giving it a little Creole tweaking, she transformed it into this delicious bayou-style appetizer. • *Yield: 6 to 8 servings*

1 tablespoon olive oil

1 dozen fresh oysters, shucked and drained of juice

1 10-ounce package frozen chopped spinach
(cooked as per package directions)

4 ounces low-fat cream cheese, softened

½ cup freshly grated Parmesan cheese

½ cup low-fat mayonnaise

½ cup fat-free sour cream

2 teaspoons freshly squeezed lemon juice

1 medium-size clove garlic, pressed in garlic press or minced

2 green onions, sliced thin

10 drops Tabasco sauce

1 tablespoon Worcestershire sauce

½ teaspoon salt, or to taste

freshly ground black pepper to taste

melba-toast rounds, for serving

1   Preheat the oven to 350 degrees.

2   Heat the olive oil in a skillet over medium heat. Cook the oysters in the oil for about 5 minutes, until their edges curl up. Remove from the heat and set them aside.

3   In a food processor or blender, combine the spinach, cream cheese, Parmesan cheese, mayonnaise, sour cream, and lemon juice.

4   Transfer the mixture to a bowl and stir in the garlic, onions, Tabasco, Worcestershire, and salt. Season with pepper. Gently fold in the oysters.

5   Spoon the mixture into a casserole or baking dish. Bake for 25 minutes, until bubbly. Serve warm with melba-toast rounds.

CREOLE CASSEROLE WITH EGGPLANT, SHRIMP, AND CRABMEAT

This dish received raves on Low-Fat Tuesday night for its layered nuances of flavors and spices. The combination of eggplant, shrimp, crabmeat, and breadcrumbs results in a very rich dish, so you may want to limit your portion size, or else plan on taking a couple of trips around the veranda after dinner. Note that crawfish tails can be substituted for the shrimp. Frozen crawfish tails can usually be found in specialty markets or fish stores. However, the first person who calls them "crayfish" has to either give away her Mardi Gras beads or do the dishes. • *Yield: 4 to 6 servings*

1 medium eggplant (about 1½ pounds)
cooking spray
1½ tablespoons canola oil
3 tablespoons flour
¾ cup skim milk
1 cup cooked shrimp, chopped
½ pound lump crabmeat
¾ cup chopped green onions
¾ cup seasoned breadcrumbs

2 teaspoons garlic, minced
1 tablespoon fresh parsley, finely chopped
⅓ cup green pepper, finely chopped
½ teaspoon paprika
½ teaspoon dried oregano
½ teaspoon dried thyme
½ teaspoon salt
¼ teaspoon cayenne pepper
¼ teaspoon freshly ground black pepper

1 Preheat the oven to 450 degrees.

2 Prick the eggplant all over with a fork. Place it on a foil-lined pan and roast it until the eggplant collapses and the skin turns brown, about 45 minutes. When done, set it aside to cool. When cool, slice it in half lengthwise and scoop out the flesh.

3 Lower the oven to 350 degrees. Spray a medium-to-large-size casserole or baking dish with cooking spray.

4 Heat the oil in a saucepan over medium-high heat. Add the flour and stir constantly with a wire whisk until it turns a deep golden brown. This is called a roux. Do not let the roux scorch. (Should it burn even slightly, discard it and begin again.)

5 Add the milk and continue stirring until it has thickened.

6 Remove from the heat, then stir in the eggplant and the remaining ingredients. Pour the mixture into the prepared dish and bake for 30 minutes. Serve warm.

BEER BISCUITS

What better way to pay homage to Mardi Gras than to include the beverage that becomes the city's most popular form of hydration during carnival—beer? For this recipe we recommend using regional beers—Dixie and Abita are two—for authenticity's sake. But frankly, any cheap beer of your choosing will result in an equally delicious beer biscuit. Note that despite their frat-boy-sounding name, they actually taste quite sophisticated; the beer gives them a subtle sweetness, making them a perfect accompaniment to the spicier dishes. Oh, and Katherine's mother will confirm that beer is, in fact, fat-free. • *Yield: 1 dozen biscuits*

4 cups self-rising flour, sifted
¼ cup sugar
16 ounces beer
1 tablespoon fresh chopped dill, or 1 teaspoon dried
1 tablespoon melted butter

1 Preheat the oven to 400 degrees.
2 Spray 12 muffin cups with nonstick spray.
3 In a large bowl mix the flour and sugar. Add the beer and dill and stir well to blend.
4 Fill the muffin cups about ¾ full. Bake for 10 minutes.
5 Remove and brush butter over the top of each biscuit. Bake for an additional 10 minutes or until golden brown.

TURKEY SAUSAGE AND CHICKEN GUMBO

As we already mentioned, gumbo is a classic regional dish that Creoles, Cajuns, and everyone in between claim as their own. Our recipe calls for lower-fat turkey sausage and chicken, though a gumbo's ingredients can include crabs, shrimp, or anything else that can be caught in the Gulf of Mexico, as well as filé powder (ground sassafras root from Africa), which is used in a filé gumbo. But while we've kept our gumbo recipe fairly simple, the flavor is far from it. Gumbo is often served over rice, but we did without it to save room for the rest of the dishes in this meal. ▪ *Yield: 6 servings*

¼ cup plus 1 tablespoon vegetable oil

4½ tablespoons flour

2 cups chopped onions

1 cup chopped celery

1 cup chopped green pepper

4 cloves garlic, minced

½ cup chopped fresh parsley

1 pound low-fat turkey sausage, sliced into 1-inch-thick rounds

3 cups chicken stock

1 cup canned stewed tomatoes

2 teaspoons cayenne pepper

1½ teaspoons dried thyme

2 pounds cooked boneless, skinless chicken breasts, diced

1 cup chopped scallions (white parts plus 3 inches of green)

salt and freshly ground black pepper to taste

1   Heat 4 tablespoons (¼ cup) of the oil in a saucepan over medium-high heat. Add the flour and stir constantly with a wire whisk until it turns dark brown. (This is a dark roux.) Do not let it scorch. (Should it burn even slightly, discard it and begin again.) Set it aside.

2   In a separate large saucepan, heat the remaining 1 tablespoon of oil over medium heat. Add the onions, celery, green pepper, garlic, parsley, and sausage. Sauté for 10 minutes, until the vegetables are tender. Add the chicken stock, tomatoes, cayenne pepper, and thyme. Bring to a rolling boil.

3   Add the roux, lower the heat, and let it simmer for 20 minutes. Add the chicken and scallions and cook for 5 minutes longer. Season with salt and pepper.

SOUTHERN COMFORT: KATHERINE, OUR RESIDENT BAYOU BELLE, STIRS IT UP FOR MARDI GRAS

OKRA AND TOMATOES

Okra and tomatoes are a Southern staple and complement the other dishes we served at this dinner well. This dish is very easy to make, and you can substitute different spices (such as curry powder), or use sautéed garlic. For a more substantial dish, you can even add other ingredients, such as green pepper and shrimp, or yellow corn and white beans. • *Yield: 4 to 6 servings*

2 tablespoons olive oil
½ cup finely chopped sweet white onions
1½ pounds fresh okra, sliced into 1-inch-thick rounds
2 firm red tomatoes, peeled, seeded, and coarsely chopped
1 firm yellow tomato, peeled, seeded, and coarsely chopped
1 teaspoon salt
1 teaspoon paprika
freshly ground black pepper to taste

1   Heat the olive oil in a skillet over medium heat. Cook the onions for about 5 minutes, until tender.

2   Add the okra. Cook uncovered for about 5 minutes, until the okra is no longer stringy, stirring occasionally.

3   Add the tomatoes and the seasonings. Cook, covered, for about 10 to 15 minutes, until the okra is tender.

NORTHERNER
CYNTHIA
ATTEMPTS TO
BRING BANANAS
FOSTER ABOVE
THE MASON-
DIXON LINE

BANANAS FOSTER WITH PRALINED PECANS

Part of what gives New Orleans food its character is that it is unabashedly "old school." (Katherine knows a family whose male members have been passing down a secret recipe for homemade Creole mayonnaise for generations. Some families have coats of arms, others, condiments.) Another example of an age-old dish is Bananas Foster. This dessert, traditionally served flambéed, originated more than fifty years ago at the famous New Orleans restaurant Brennan's, and is named after Mr. Foster, a regular patron. The traditional recipe includes ingredients that would never pass muster with today's nutrition experts—well, except for the bananas. What follows, however, is a much lighter version of the traditional Foster sauce, to which we've added pralined pecans to give it a crunchy pizzazz. To cut additional calories from the original, serve it with frozen yogurt instead of ice cream. The result is so heavenly, we'll bet even Mr. Foster would come back for more. ▪ *Yield: 4 to 6 servings*

FOR THE PRALINED PECANS:
1½ tablespoons light brown sugar
½ tablespoon butter
2 teaspoons water
⅔ cup whole pecans

FOR THE BANANAS FOSTER SAUCE:
½ cup firmly packed light brown sugar
4 teaspoons cornstarch
½ cup cold water
1 tablespoon butter
2 tablespoons rum
1½ teaspoons vanilla extract
3 medium-size bananas, sliced into
½-inch rounds
1 pint low-fat vanilla frozen yogurt

1   To prepare the pralined pecans, stir the light brown sugar, butter, and water together in a small saucepan over medium heat until the sugar has dissolved. Bring to a boil, then let it simmer, stirring frequently, until the sauce has thickened, about 2 to 3 minutes. Add the pecans; stir until well coated. Spoon the pecans onto wax paper and let them cool.

2   To prepare the sauce, add the light brown sugar, cornstarch, and water to a saucepan. Cook over medium-high heat, stirring constantly, until the mixture begins to boil. Boil for 1 minute.

3   Reduce the heat to low, stir in the butter, rum, and vanilla, and cook until the butter is melted. Stir in the bananas; simmer for 2 minutes.

4   While still warm, spoon the bananas and sauce over individual servings of frozen yogurt. Sprinkle the cooled pecans on top of each serving.

CREMA DI POMODORO
(FRESH TOMATO SOUP)

quick

BAKED ARTICHOKE DIP

CREMA DI POMODORO
(FRESH TOMATO SOUP)

RED PEPPER AND
GOAT CHEESE FLAT BREADS

THE EASIEST APRICOT CHICKEN

ROSEMARY
POTATO CHIPS

ALL-AMERICAN APPLE PIE

the quick fix

DINNER FASTER THAN YOU CAN SAY "TEN ITEMS OR LESS"

QUICK & EASY NIGHT TAKES SHAPE OVER E-MAIL:

lucia: what did you make for dinner last night?

becky: reservations.

sharon: are we still on for sunday night? i'm in a wedding this weekend and i'm not sure i'll have time to cook.

katherine: oooh . . . what color is the dress?

sharon: teal raw silk.

lisa: sharon, i know i speak for the group when i say we're sorry.

cynthia: what if we made quick dishes?

becky: like toast?

On very rare instances (think solar eclipse), cooking on Sundays has crimped CC's style. And so one October, fall fell— and so did the six of us, for six different men. Yes, in a Cooking Club first, we were all in love at the very same time, and these burgeoning relationships meant that Sunday spent wandering around SoHo with the new beau was suddenly preferable to a hot date with the stove.

In the past, when we had pondered what could tear our supper club apart—mandatory citrus consumption, carnivorous condescension, a burnt bundt—the only real threat that loomed was the thought of rescheduling. But now this conviction to meet come hell or high water suddenly seemed as firm as a three-week-old carrot. Cancellation seemed to foreshadow dissolution: It would just lead to a slippery slope of procrastination, conflicting schedules, ingredients gone bad. We were in desperate need of some culinary Cliff's Notes— and the future of our club depended on it.

For the long-term good of Cooking Club, we decided that

we could cut a few corners just this once. We'd pare down the purism, sanction super-market substitutes, and eliminate unnecessary ingredients. The goal was to produce food that required minimal culinary commitment, tasted great, and still let us get to dinner on time. Not to mention that easy-to-prepare recipes would be a welcome addition to the repertoire for nights when members found themselves hungry and alone.

If cooking becomes an Olympic sport, these super-speedy recipes may make it to the qualifying trials. The results proved so fast, even Lisa made it to dinner on time. And an apricot chicken and rosemary potato chips dinner was recently served on a weeknight in the Fredman home—an astounding fact when you consider that its preparation was preceded by a trip to the gym, and that the dishes were done before *Will and Grace*.

This culinary ode of minimalism did raise a few ethical dilemmas: Is it cheating to use ready-made piecrusts? Does incorporating ingredients like store-bought roasted red peppers constitute fraud? Our voter polling came in as a definitive NO. Cooking doesn't always have to mean slaving over a stove and making everything from scratch. The artichoke dip, however, presented a more delicate issue. Is the chef obliged to tell guests who are busy scarfing down dip-laden pita triangles by the bushel that the secret ingredient is (gasp) plain old mayonnaise? After some debate, one member said that she would come clean (there are worse things), while the duplicitous majority agreed on either (a) a quick-and-breezy conversation change, or (b) a little white lie ("It's a fat-free yogurt-based spread with antioxidant properties").

The success of our night doesn't mean that we'll stop ordering in Chinese food (a girl needs her dim sum). Or that we won't enjoy a good bowl of Cheerios now and then (with ten essential vitamins and minerals, its nutritional content could challenge that of spinach). But we did find the middle road between mei fun and Martha to be well worth the trip.

BAKED ARTICHOKE DIP

Buying canned artichoke hearts is the best way to save time. (If you don't believe us, ask any-one who has ever tried to machete their way to a fresh artichoke heart.) For those of you who may have nightmares about using three quarters of a cup of mayo in one dip (Sharon has lost many a night's sleep over this), use the reduced-fat variety. • *Yield: 4 to 6 servings*

2 14-ounce cans artichoke hearts, drained and chopped
¾ cup mayonnaise
¾ cup Parmesan cheese
salt and freshly ground black pepper to taste
pita chips or crackers, for serving

I   Preheat the oven to 350 degrees.
2   Place the artichoke hearts in a large bowl. Add the mayonnaise and Parmesan cheese and mix with a fork to combine the ingredients. Season with salt and pepper.
3   Put the mixture into a baking dish (preferably one that can be used to serve, to avoid having to transfer the dip to a decorative plate). Bake for about 25 minutes, until the top is golden brown. Serve warm with pita chips or crackers.

CREMA DI POMODORO
(FRESH TOMATO SOUP)

This soup is a renegade from our Italian night because it couldn't be easier. You don't even have to peel the tomatoes. At a small restaurant we know of in Florence, this soup is made to order in a blender behind the bar and served immediately. We also like it chilled before serving. ▪ *Yield: 4 to 6 servings*

8 ripe tomatoes, quartered and seeded

¾ cup loosely packed fresh basil leaves,
plus additional for garnish

¼ cup olive oil, plus additional for garnish

salt and freshly ground black pepper to taste

4 thin slices fresh mozzarella, cut into 3 strips

1   In a blender, combine half of the tomatoes with the basil, olive oil, salt, and pepper. Blend until the volume is reduced, then add the remaining tomatoes. Blend on high at least 1 minute, until the mixture is fully blended, smooth, and frothy.

2   Pour into bowls, top with the mozzarella strips, and drizzle with oil. Garnish each soup with a leaf or two of additional basil. If you wish, chill the ungarnished soup in the refrigerator before serving.

RED PEPPER AND GOAT CHEESE FLAT BREADS

Roasting red peppers involves peeling charred skin, so save time and prevent burned fingers by opening a jar of the supermarket substitutes. Since all the ingredients end up in the blender, even your picky mother-in-law will not be able to distinguish the difference. To save even more time, use seasoned flat breads to add extra flavor without any extra effort. • *Yield: 6 servings*

1 13-ounce jar roasted peppers packed in oil
1 teaspoon garlic powder
salt and freshly ground black pepper to taste
4 ounces softened goat cheese
1 box seasoned flat breads
crushed red pepper flakes (optional)

1   In a blender mix the red peppers with their oil, garlic powder, salt, and pepper. Make sure not to overblend in order to retain some texture.

2   Spread a generous amount of goat cheese on the flat breads, then top with the red-pepper mixture. Sprinkle crushed red pepper flakes on top, if desired.

DON'T BLINK OR YOU'LL MISS CHEF CYN'S SUPER-SPEEDY FLATBREAD PREP

THE EASIEST APRICOT CHICKEN

This chicken recipe has become a staple in the Fredman home. And because it is the only meal Sharon makes after work, by default it's her husband, Ken's, favorite dinner. But since he is just so happy to get a home-cooked meal, he doesn't even care that after all the time Sharon spends making food for her cooking club, all he gets is a dish that takes almost no time to prepare. ▪ *Yield: 4 to 6 servings*

2 18-ounce jars apricot preserves
1 12-ounce jar Dijon mustard
3 pounds boneless, skinless chicken breasts

1   Preheat the oven to 350 degrees.
2   In a large bowl, combine the apricot preserves and the mustard. (If you want this to be less spicy, add less mustard. The ratio should be based on your tastes.)
3   Cut the chicken breasts into strips about 2 inches wide and add to the apricot mixture. Generously coat the chicken.
4   Pour the chicken and the sauce into a baking dish and cook for about 45 minutes.

ROSEMARY POTATO CHIPS

This recipe sounds too simple to taste this good, but just a hint of rosemary and other seasonings baked onto the potato adds a lot of unexpected flavor. The "chips" come out the crispiest when baked on a cookie sheet. • *Yield: 6 servings*

cooking spray

6 baking potatoes, washed and scrubbed well,
and cut into ½-inch-thick round slices

2 tablespoons olive oil

¼ cup dried rosemary

1 tablespoon garlic powder

2 tablespoons dried oregano

salt and freshly ground black pepper to taste

1   Preheat the oven to 350 degrees.

2   Spray a cookie sheet with cooking spray.

3   Place the potato slices in a bowl and toss with the olive oil, making sure all slices are coated. Then add the seasonings, making sure each piece of potato gets a generous supply of the rosemary, garlic powder, oregano, salt, and pepper.

4   Place the slices on the prepared cookie sheet. Cook for about 45 minutes, until the potatoes are crispy.

QUICK & EASY

TO SHARON,
"QUICK AND
EASY" MEANS
SKIPPING
SUPERMARKET
LINES FOR THE
CORNER DELI

ALL-AMERICAN APPLE PIE

By using cornstarch instead of flour and brushing the bottom and top crusts with an egg-white mixture, this recipe is the quickest way to a perfectly prepared pie. But when your guests ask you for your secret piecrust recipe, just smile and mumble something about your great-great-grandmother. ▪ *Yield: 1 pie*

> **8 apples (Golden Delicious, Braeburn, or Granny Smith),**
> **peeled, cored, and sliced 1 inch thick**
> **¾ cup sugar**
> **1 teaspoon cinnamon**
> **1½ tablespoons cornstarch**
> **2 Pillsbury prepared piecrusts (dough available in the**
> **refrigerator section of your supermarket)**
> **egg wash (1 egg white beaten with 1 tablespoon water)**

1 Preheat the oven to 350 degrees.

2 Place the apple slices in a large bowl and toss them with the sugar, cinnamon, and cornstarch.

3 Place one of the piecrusts in a 9-inch pie dish and brush the bottom and sides with the egg wash. Add the apple filling.

4 Put the second piecrust on top and pinch the edges together decoratively. Brush the rest of the egg wash on top of the piecrust.

5 Cook for about 1 hour. Important: Let the pie cool for at least 2 hours before serving. It can be left overnight and then served at room temperature or reheated the next day.

QUICK & EASY

CELLOPHANE NOODLE SALAD WITH SHRIMP

asian

MENU

CELLOPHANE NOODLE SALAD
WITH SHRIMP

SHIITAKE DUMPLINGS

THAI VEGETABLE CURRY

SPICY PEANUT CHICKEN

LEMONGRASS BASS

COCONUT RICE PUDDING

far east feast

DISHES TO FILL OUR BUDDHA BELLIES

ASIAN NIGHT TAKES SHAPE OVER E-MAIL:

becky: so, i'm thinking about picking up some "special" fortune cookies from the restaurant on the corner to spice up asian night.

lucia: ah, yes, the dirty fortune cookies! you ask the waiter and he says "regular . . . or *special*?" with that knowing nod. i suppose if we were real chefs we would make our own.

lisa: confucius say: you are best cook in club.

cynthia: man don't like your special delights, you drop him like hot wonton.

sharon: you will sleep with full belly tonight.

becky: confucius say: tofutti go right to your booty.

katherine: confucius say: lucia bought her dish at zabar's.

In the early eighties, when we were busy trading stickers and pining for Duran Duran, chicken and broccoli was the only Asian dish we had ever tasted. And the only sushi eater we knew was Molly Ringwald in *The Breakfast Club.* We grew up, and so did our taste buds. Living in New York, you quickly develop an aptitude for the subtleties of Asian cuisine not otherwise found this side of the Himalayas. Denizens of the Big Apple can have Thai, Korean, or Vietnamese delivered as easily as a large pepperoni with extra cheese. Super-speedy sushi has replaced the brown-bag lunch. And hot new restaurants often sport Pan-Asian fusion themes that are as fleeting as the season's hemline.

While many New Yorkers can recognize sizzling Korean *bibimbop* three tables away, ask them how to cook it and they'll look at you like you're a Komodo dragon. But preparing Eastern cuisine doesn't have to be complicated. Most supermarkets now carry the requisite ingredients: Coconut milk, fish sauce, and sesame oil can be found just down the aisle from the canned corn and Wheaties. And once you've mastered the basics, root out an Asian specialty store and explore the uses of rice paper, cellophane noodles, and seaweed. Before you know it, you'll be running over treetops with your Ginsu knife.

In addition, get to know the exotic world of rice. Jasmine, basmati, and sticky are some of the most common varieties, but venture into Thai black or Bhutanese red rice, and you won't just be thinking side dish anymore. Even if you have only the good old American white stuff on hand, add coconut milk in place of some of the water while cooking, and send Uncle Ben on an instant holiday to Chiang Mai. The flavorful rice that results can be an aromatic base for any Thai-inspired dish, like the curry vegetables and peanut chicken we've included here. And remember, when in doubt, sprinkle chopped peanuts on top.

We've had several Asian nights, and they've been some of our best. Instead of focusing our efforts on one country, we always choose to run wild over the region—because the dishes somehow always seem to work well together. At the last one we took advantage of what we think is the coolest wedding gift we've seen yet: Sharon's fifty-piece sushi-rolling set (the matching his-and-hers aprons were a bit much, though). And Lisa, never intimidated by seemingly labor-intensive dishes, assured us that making dumplings is a cinch. We believe her now. (See Shiitake Dumplings, page 114.)

The only place where we've been let down is in the Asian dessert category. Cynthia lives smack in the middle of Little Italy and Chinatown, and after a thorough investigation, the verdict is in: Gelato beats red bean paste any day. But before you skip straight to the Italian chapter, give the Coconut Rice Pudding a try. It's the one dessert we actually like, 'cause who knew pineapple chunks on toothpicks were no longer the only option?

CELLOPHANE NOODLE SALAD WITH SHRIMP

This cold Vietnamese salad has a slightly sweet dressing that we love. Cellophane noodles, made from mung bean flour, don't need to be cooked, just softened in hot water until they become transparent. If your grocery store doesn't carry cellophane noodles, try an Asian specialty market. If you can't track them down, rice noodles or thin spaghetti (cooked according to the directions on the package) will work as well. • *Yield: 4 to 6 servings*

FOR THE DRESSING:

2 cloves garlic, minced

¼ cup rice wine vinegar

⅓ cup Asian fish sauce

4 scallions, chopped (white parts plus 2 inches of green)

½ teaspoon chili paste

2 tablespoons lime juice

1 tablespoon sesame oil

3 tablespoons sugar

FOR THE SALAD:

½ pound cellophane noodles
(rice noodles or thin spaghetti can be substituted)

1 pound (about 20) precooked large peeled shrimp
(heads and tails removed)

1 large carrot, peeled, halved, and julienned

1 cucumber, peeled, halved, seeded, and julienned

3 heaping tablespoons cilantro leaves

2 tablespoons black sesame seeds

1   In a bowl, combine the dressing ingredients and whisk until well blended. Refrigerate until cold.

2   In a separate bowl soak the noodles in hot water until softened. Rinse with cold water and drain. (If you're using any other type of noodle, follow the cooking instructions on the package, then rinse with cold water and drain.)

3   In a large bowl, combine the salad ingredients and gently toss with the chilled dressing.

CYNTHIA HITS
CHINATOWN FOR
AUTHENTIC RICES
AND SPICES

SHIITAKE DUMPLINGS

When it comes to Chinese take-out, we realized that steamed vegetable dumplings are on all of our top ten most-ordered lists. So we decided to see just how difficult they are to make by hand. Finding the wrappers is the hardest part (you may have to go to an Asian market), but we're happy to report that Chinese cabbage has found its way into many a supermarket. We found that the key to a good vegetable dumpling is that, unlike a meat dumpling, it needs texture—so if you are using a food processor do not overprocess or the mixture will become a paste. ▪ *Yield: 22 dumplings*

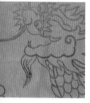

FOR THE DUMPLINGS:

1 tablespoon sesame oil

2 cloves garlic, minced

½ pound shiitake mushrooms, stems removed, cleaned, and sliced

½ cup chopped Chinese or Napa cabbage

½ cup chopped carrots

1 tablespoon soy sauce

1 package round gyoza dumpling wrappers (available in Asian markets)

FOR THE DIPPING SAUCE:

¼ cup soy sauce

1 tablespoon rice wine vinegar (regular red wine vinegar may be substituted)

1 teaspoon sesame oil

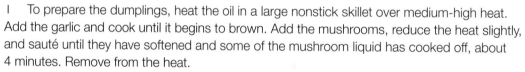

1   To prepare the dumplings, heat the oil in a large nonstick skillet over medium-high heat. Add the garlic and cook until it begins to brown. Add the mushrooms, reduce the heat slightly, and sauté until they have softened and some of the mushroom liquid has cooked off, about 4 minutes. Remove from the heat.

2   Place the cabbage, carrots, mushroom mixture, and soy sauce in a food processor and give about 10 quick pulses to chop the ingredients to a mince.

3   Place a small mound of filling in the middle of each dumpling wrapper. Fold half of the wrapper over the mound to form a half-moon shape, then wet the edges with a bit of water to seal.

4   Steam the dumplings in a steamer until the wrappers are soft and translucent, about 5 to 10 minutes, depending on the thickness.

5   While the dumplings are cooking, prepare the dipping sauce. Combine the three ingredients and whisk them together. Serve alongside the dumplings.

DUMPLINGS ARE EVEN MORE FUN TO MAKE WHILE EXPLAINING THE PROCESS TO AN IMAGINARY COOKING-SHOW AUDIENCE

THAI VEGETABLE CURRY

Yes, this recipe has more ingredients than the entire Quick Fix chapter, but cook up some rice and you've got a one-course Asian dinner. The cilantro, basil, and peanut garnish at the end is guaranteed to impress even your most aesthetically-minded clubmates. • *Yield: 4 to 6 servings*

1 small eggplant (about 1 pound)

1 teaspoon salt, plus additional for salting eggplant

1 pound (approximately 4 loose cups) string beans, stem ends removed and cut in half

1/4 cup vegetable oil

3 cloves garlic, peeled and sliced

1 large onion, peeled and diced

2 red peppers, cut into 1/2-inch cubes

2 teaspoons minced fresh gingerroot

1/2 cup chopped fresh basil

1/2 cup chopped fresh cilantro

1 cup canned chicken or vegetable stock

1 cup canned coconut milk

2 tablespoons fresh lime juice

2 tablespoons tomato paste

1/2 teaspoon crushed red pepper flakes

1/4 teaspoon ground cumin

6 cups cooked rice

1 cup chopped peanuts

1   Cut the eggplant into 1/2-inch-thick slices. To cut the eggplant's bitter taste, sprinkle both sides of each slice with salt and let them sit in a colander for at least 30 minutes. Rinse the eggplant and squeeze the excess water from it through a clean dishtowel.

2   Using a vegetable steamer, steam the string beans for 3 to 5 minutes, stirring once, until they are bright green and still crisp. (If you do not have a steamer, you may drop the beans in boiling water for 2 to 3 minutes, then proceed.) Remove and douse in a bowl of ice water. Drain and set aside.

3   In a large saucepan over medium-high heat, heat the oil. Sauté the garlic and onion until translucent, about 3 to 4 minutes.

4   Add the eggplant and peppers and continue to cook for about 5 minutes.

5   Add the ginger, 1/4 cup of basil, 1/4 cup of cilantro, stock, coconut milk, lime juice, tomato paste, red pepper flakes, cumin, and salt, cover, and simmer for 35 minutes, stirring occasionally. Add the string beans for the last 5 minutes of cooking.

6   Serve over rice, and garnish with chopped peanuts and the remaining chopped basil and cilantro.

SPICY PEANUT CHICKEN

This dish has a strange power—it will send your guests into the kitchen to scrape the Teflon coating of your pan, trying to get any leftover sauce. Or so it has been for us on more than one occasion. We recommend not letting people serve themselves this dish, and don't use your good pots. ▪ *Yield: 4 to 6 servings*

6 scallions, diced (white parts plus 2 inches of green)

1 teaspoon fresh ginger, minced

3 tablespoons soy sauce

5 heaping tablespoons peanut butter

1 cup water

¼ to ½ teaspoon crushed red pepper flakes

1 teaspoon brown sugar

1 tablespoon sesame oil

1½ pound thinly sliced boneless, skinless chicken breasts, cut into strips

6 cups cooked rice or noodles

¾ cup chopped peanuts

1   To prepare the sauce, in a bowl combine the scallions, ginger, soy sauce, peanut butter, water, red pepper flakes, and brown sugar. Whisk until smooth.

2   In a large nonstick pan, heat the sesame oil over medium-high heat and sauté the chicken breasts until golden, about 4 minutes per side, then remove from the pan.

3   Add the sauce to the pan and cook until it begins to simmer. Turn heat down slightly and continue to simmer, stirring occasionally, for an additional 5 minutes, until the sauce begins to thicken.

4   Return the chicken to the pan and cook for about 2 minutes, or until the chicken is cooked through.

5   Serve over rice or noodles and sprinkle with the chopped peanuts.

ASIAN

LEMONGRASS BASS

We like names that rhyme, and we also like tasty fish dishes. This Cambodian-inspired recipe combines both, and comes courtesy of a CC boyfriend with a culinary prowess we find threatening. If you don't happen to have any galangal root or sake lying around (as most of us don't), the ginger and wine substitutions work well. • *Yield: 4 to 6 servings*

4 tablespoons salted butter

5 stalks lemongrass, peeled to soft inner core and minced

½ cup minced galangal root, or ¼ cup minced fresh ginger

2 cups dry sake or white wine

salt and freshly ground black pepper to taste

2 ripe tomatoes, seeded and diced

⅓ cup basil leaves, chopped

4 sea bass fillets (6 to 8 ounces each)

1   Preheat the oven to 425 degrees.

2   In a medium saucepan, melt 2 tablespoons of the butter over medium-low heat (do not brown). Add the lemongrass and galangal and gently sauté (no browning) for about 5 minutes, until soft.

3   Add the sake, salt, and pepper. Bring to a boil, then reduce the heat and simmer the sauce to reduce for about 5 minutes.

4   Remove the pan from the heat and strain the sauce. Discard the lemongrass and ginger (if using) and return the sauce to the pan.

5   Stir in the tomatoes and basil and simmer for 2 more minutes, then remove from the heat.

6   Place the sea bass fillets individually on 4 sheets of aluminum foil. Spoon the sauce over the fillets, place ½ tablespoon of butter on top of each, and completely seal the packets, leaving air pockets inside so that the fish can steam. Bake in the oven for 30 minutes. Remove, open the packets, and serve.

COCONUT RICE PUDDING

Yum. We love rice pudding, and this one's delicate spices make it glam enough for a dinner party. You can adjust the amount of milk you add at the end depending on whether you like your pudding thick or thin. • *Yield: 4 to 6 servings*

2½ cups water

¼ teaspoon salt

1 cup Thai jasmine rice, or medium- or long-grained white rice

1 14-ounce can coconut milk

½ cup sugar

⅓ cup raisins

½ teaspoon vanilla extract

½ teaspoon ground cardamom

½ teaspoon ground cinnamon

½ teaspoon ground nutmeg

2 cups milk

1   In a medium saucepan, bring the water and salt to a boil. Add the rice, lower the heat, and simmer, covered, for 20 minutes or until the rice is tender.

2   In a large saucepan, combine the coconut milk, sugar, raisins, vanilla, and spices, and stir until the sugar has dissolved and the mixture begins to bubble.

3   Add the cooked rice and continue to simmer, uncovered, over low heat for 15 to 20 minutes, stirring occasionally, until the rice is thick and creamy but is not sticking to the bottom of the saucepan.

4   Add the milk and continue to simmer, stirring occasionally, an additional 15 to 20 minutes, until the pudding reaches the desired consistency.

ASIAN

MANGO SMOOTHIE AND
BANANA BLUEBERRY MUFFINS

brunch

MENU

ARUGULA BLUEBERRY SALAD
WITH ORANGE DRESSING

POTATO FRITTATA

BANANA BLUEBERRY MUFFINS

BANKA'S DUTCH PANCAKES
WITH STRAWBERRIES

GREEN EGGS AND BACON

MANGO SMOOTHIE

sleeping in

BREAKFAST FOR ANY TIME OF DAY

BREAKFAST ALL DAY TAKES SHAPE OVER E-MAIL:

lisa: did anyone ever eat pancakes for dinner growing up?

cynthia: is that like a backwards meal?

katherine: no, that's when you eat dessert first. i think she's talking about eating breakfast for dinner.

sharon: i have problems with sweet before savory.

cynthia: i get stuck in the french-toast-versus-eggs divide.

lisa: we'll have both, but since brunch is breakfast and lunch, let's meet earlier than usual. how's four?

lucia: four P.M.? that's more like lunch and dinner—it's dunch.

lisa: dunch?

becky: i don't care what we call it, as long as there's bacon.

Brunch in New York is a competitive sport. It's as if the entire city sleeps shamefully late, and then, on cue, lines up at a handful of restaurants that serve the breakfast foods we crave. Our yen for blueberry pancakes, zucchini muffins, and eggs any way we want them leads to a forty-five-minute wait for a table, a forty-five-dollar check, and reentry into Sunday afternoon just before dark. Fed up—and underfed—we decided to take brunch into our own hands, and make breakfast for dinner.

Brunch turned out to be a sweet and savory bonanza. We made herbed scrambled eggs (which could be kept warm in the oven for the chronically late), and fashioned a lattice of cooked bacon over the top, which the vegetarians among us could easily peel off. (It should be noted that we witnessed at least one longtime herbivore succumb to her inner Homer Simpson and gobble some up.) You can also serve them with warm tortillas and salsa for a gringa gal's take on huevos rancheros.

Lisa brought a frittata because she believes that real women don't eat quiche. The frittata has all the makings of a staple brunch food: It's hearty, it's starchy, and it can be eaten with ketchup or Tabasco (for the Advanced Placement brunch participants). This one is a standard potato-and-egg number, but it's easy to layer in other ingredients, such as sautéed spinach or diced tomatoes. Because you can never have too many carbs at brunch, we also served Dutch pancakes, a secret recipe of Becky's in-laws. (She had to marry into the family before they'd fork over the recipe.) These wafer-thin treats are a close relative of the crepe—even closer to a blintz, if you've ever eaten one. These, too, can be kept warm in the oven for tardy guests.

If you read the fine print on the food pyramid, there's a little-known rule that says that on Sundays you should chase protein and starch with more protein and starch, fortified with sugar. Any quick bread or muffin will do; we like the granola-topped Banana Blueberry Muffins that follow. And lest you think we were removed from Becky's apartment with a crane, you should know that we served both fruit (in the form of a sunny Mango Smoothie) and vegetables. Our colorful salad combines unexpected ingredients, such as sweet blueberries, tart arugula, and buttery avocado, with an orange dressing that's mild enough to eat before noon.

Because it's easy to prepare brunch foods ahead of time, this is the ideal meal for an initial foray into group entertaining—never mind that expectations on a Sunday morning are dramatically lower than they would have been fifteen hours earlier. (Though a bowl of Honey Nut Cheerios can be tough competition at times, as long as there's enough food, brunch guests will usually be happy. Just don't forget to caffeinate the cranky ones.) Plus there's the added bonus that if disaster strikes, it's easy to improvise (e.g., "I just burned the muffins! Cynthia, bring over your crepe pan!"). And breakfast begs for buffet style: Guests want to try a little bit of everything and reserve the right to go back for seconds (or, in the case of bacon, thirds). And finally, buy a bottle of champagne. In the event of a culinary crisis, mix with orange juice and serve multiple rounds.

ARUGULA BLUEBERRY SALAD
WITH ORANGE DRESSING

This colorful dish has been a fixture at the New York City bridal-shower-brunch circuit for at least five years now. (If you don't have time to make the dressing—though it's really worth the extra five minutes—we've heard that Newman's Own olive oil and vinegar dressing is an acceptable substitute.) ▪ *Yield: 4 to 6 servings*

FOR THE SALAD:

1 head Boston lettuce, rinsed well and dried
2 bunches arugula, rinsed well and dried
2 Hass avocados, peeled, pitted, and cubed
4 plum tomatoes, chopped
1 pint blueberries
1 can hearts of palm, drained and cut into ¼-inch-thick rounds

FOR THE DRESSING:

½ cup freshly squeezed orange juice
2 tablespoons fresh lime juice
½ teaspoon finely grated orange zest
½ teaspoon sugar
¼ teaspoon salt
⅓ cup olive oil

1   Use a kitchen knife to shred the Boston lettuce and the arugula into ½-inch strips. Set aside.

2   To prepare the dressing, whisk together the orange and lime juices, orange zest, sugar, and salt. While whisking with one hand, drizzle the olive oil into the mixture with the other, and continue to whisk until well blended.

3   Just before serving the salad, toss about half of the dressing with the greens to coat. Add the remaining salad ingredients, and dress to taste with the rest of the vinaigrette.

THE BONUS OF
BREAKFAST AT
FOUR? WE'RE HALF
AS CRANKY AND
TWICE AS HUNGRY

POTATO FRITTATA

In Spain this dish is often called a tortilla, or a potato omelet. You can layer in different cooked ingredients instead of the potatoes, such as sliced, cooked mushrooms or spinach. The best thing about this dish is that, like pizza, it tastes great cold, warm, or at room temperature.
▪ *Yield: 4 to 6 servings*

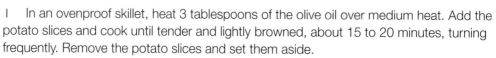

4 tablespoons olive oil

2 medium Yukon Gold potatoes, peeled and thinly sliced
(about ¼ inch thick)

1 medium onion, thinly sliced

6 eggs

2 tablespoons freshly grated Parmesan cheese

½ teaspoon salt

¼ teaspoon freshly ground black pepper

salsa for serving (optional)

chopped parsley for garnish (optional)

1   In an ovenproof skillet, heat 3 tablespoons of the olive oil over medium heat. Add the potato slices and cook until tender and lightly browned, about 15 to 20 minutes, turning frequently. Remove the potato slices and set them aside.

2   Add the remaining tablespoon of olive oil to the original skillet. Add the onion and cook over medium heat until translucent, about 4 to 5 minutes. Place the cooked potatoes in the pan in a circular pattern and cook for an additional minute.

3   In a bowl, whisk together the eggs, Parmesan cheese, salt, and pepper. Pour the mixture into the skillet. Shake the skillet a bit so that the eggs go between the potato layers. Cover and cook until the eggs are almost set (but still runny on top), about 8 to 10 minutes.

4   Put the entire pan under the broiler for 5 minutes to cook the top. Remove from the oven. Run a spatula around the edges to loosen the frittata, and slide it onto a plate. Serve with salsa and garnish with parsley, if desired.

BANANA BLUEBERRY MUFFINS

Because the blueberries and bananas add so much flavor and sweetness, this recipe requires less sugar than most muffins. We used half whole wheat flour so that we could justify eating more than three each. (It's practically health food, people!) ▪ *Yield: 1 dozen medium-sized muffins*

1 cup white flour

1 cup whole wheat flour

½ cup sugar

¼ teaspoon salt

1 tablespoon baking powder

2 eggs

2 very ripe bananas (1 mashed, 1 diced)

½ cup milk

1 teaspoon vanilla

5 tablespoons unsalted butter, melted and cooled

¾ cup blueberries (picked over to remove stems)

granola to sprinkle on top (optional)

1 Preheat the oven to 350 degrees. Line a muffin pan with paper liners, or grease well.

2 Combine the flours, sugar, salt, and baking powder in a bowl. Set aside.

3 In a separate bowl, use a mixer to blend the eggs, mashed banana, milk, vanilla, and butter.

4 Add the dry ingredients to the wet ones, and stir by hand until just moistened. Do not overmix.

5 Fold in the blueberries and diced banana. Pour the mixture into the prepared pan. Sprinkle granola on top if desired.

6 Bake for 25 to 30 minutes, or until a toothpick inserted into the center of a muffin comes out clean.

BANKA'S DUTCH PANCAKES WITH STRAWBERRIES

Because Becky's apartment boasts both a dinner table and a dishwasher, the club often parks there on Sunday nights. As a result, her husband, Steve, has broken bread with Cooking Club on the nights when he couldn't rummage enough buddies for a poker game. For our brunch, he let us in on his grandfather's secret recipe. We filled our pancakes with strawberries, but they're also delicious with raspberry jam, melted chocolate, or butter and brown sugar. • *Yield: 9 to 11 pancakes*

FOR THE FILLING:
1 tablespoon fresh lemon juice
1 tablespoon sugar
1 pint strawberries, hulled and cut in quarters

FOR THE PANCAKES:
1½ cups flour
¼ teaspoon salt
5 teaspoons sugar
1½ cups milk
5 eggs
powdered sugar to top pancakes

1   In a bowl, mix the filling ingredients together, then set them aside to sit for 15 minutes.

2   Mix all the pancake ingredients together in a blender, or in a bowl using a hand mixer.

3   Heat an 8-inch nonstick skillet over medium heat until drops of water sizzle on it. Pour about ⅓ cup of the mixture into the pan, and swirl to coat the entire bottom evenly.

4   Fry the pancake until it is almost cooked through (but not brown), about 2 minutes. Flip the pancake over to cook the other side lightly, about 30 seconds.

5   Slide the pancake onto a plate, place 2 tablespoons of the strawberry filling inside, and serve rolled up like a tortilla. Top with powdered sugar.

GREEN EGGS AND BACON

Apparently, scrambling eggs is a science. Most cooks agree that they must be cooked slowly over low heat, but that's where the similarities end. Some experts, like our friend and breakfast guru, David McLean, say that the eggs are called scrambled because a cook is supposed to be stirring them the entire time. This technique may leave you with more defined triceps, but not an entirely different dish. Since this recipe calls for eight eggs, we let them cook and set for a bit, and then start stirring. • *Yield: 4 to 6 servings*

8 eggs
2 tablespoons light cream
½ teaspoon salt
¼ teaspoon pepper
2 teaspoons fresh dill, minced
2 teaspoons fresh chives, minced
2 teaspoons fresh parsley, minced
1 tablespoon butter
8 slices bacon, cooked (optional)

1   In a bowl, whisk together the eggs, light cream, salt, pepper, and herbs.

2   Heat the butter in a skillet over low heat until melted. Pour the egg mixture into the skillet and cook over low heat. When it starts to set (after about 3 minutes), begin to stir often, until the eggs are done, about 5 to 6 more minutes.

3   If desired, garnish with bacon, weaving the pieces in a lattice over the plate of eggs.

LISA LEARNS TO MANGO: TO SKIN THIS SLIPPERY FRUIT, CUT AWAY THE SKIN FIRST, THEN CONTINUE TO SLICE PIECES UNTIL YOU HIT THE LARGE, THIN OVAL PIT

MANGO SMOOTHIE

We actually once held a smoothie night, complete with separate blenders to prevent a rumble between the lactose-intolerant and the citrophobes. This smoothie turned out to be the shake that united us—its dairy-free creamy taste and nonacidic quality satisfied both camps. Depending on the size of your blender, you may need to make this recipe in two batches. • *Yield: 4 to 6 servings*

8 ounces freshly squeezed orange juice
3 ripe bananas, sliced
2 mangoes, cubed
2 cups ice (about 12 cubes)

Place the juice, bananas, mangoes, and ice in a 40-ounce blender and liquefy.

BRUNCH

RIGATONI ALL'AMATRICIANA

italian

MENU

PANZANELLA
(BREAD SALAD)

RISOTTO WITH
TALEGGIO AND PEARS

RIGATONI ALL'AMATRICIANA

PESCE ALL'ACQUA PAZZA
("FISH IN CRAZY WATER")

BRUTTI MA BUÒNI
("UGLY BUT GOOD") COOKIES

SGROPPINO
(LEMON DESSERT SHAKE)

chow bella

LIKE TRUE RENAISSANCE WOMEN, WE MASTER SIX REGIONAL DISHES

ITALIAN NIGHT TAKES SHAPE OVER E-MAIL:

becky: why is it that foods sound so much better in italian? i'd so much rather eat *linguine al pomodoro* than spaghetti with tomato sauce.

lucia: the same is true for italian men. i could swoon over an alberto, but the name albert just doesn't do it for me.

katherine: i knew a fabio once.

cynthia: did he tear your corset off on a riverbank?

katherine: alas, no.

sharon: i don't like men whose hair is longer than mine.

lisa: or who dress better than i do.

katherine: how did you know i own a corset?

At first, the idea of Italian night seemed too easy. Been there, done that, we all know what's for dinner. After all, too much pasta with tomato sauce was one of the reasons why we started our club in the first place. But Cynthia, who had spent the better part of a college semester in Italy, and Lucia, whose family archives we were anxious to explore, pushed us past the spaghetti-and-meatball mind-set. For example, when Cynthia arrived in Padua expecting to overdose on pasta, she discovered that rice and polenta were the carbs of choice in Northern Italy. With the variety of regional cuisines in Italy, eating your way through the whole country could take a year's worth of club meetings. A tasty idea, come to think of it.

Most cities in Italy have a specialty, and Italians take pride in knowing who does what best. For example, a true Italian knows that Genoa is home to the best pesto and Bologna is known for tortellini. Unfortunately for Cynthia, Padua's was *cavallo*—horse meat. Whether or not they know how to cook (chances are they do), most Italians have an opinion about the perfect *pasta al pomodoro,* or whether Illy or Lavazza coffee delivers a superior cup of espresso. And unless you have an afternoon to while away in a piazza, don't get them started on the best olive oil, pasta, or, God forbid, soccer team. This is, after all, a country that shuts down for two hours in the middle of the day for lunch.

But the real beauty of Italian food is its simplicity. Some of the most elegant Italian dishes list only a handful of ingredients. The simpler the recipe, however, the more its success depends on the quality of what you put in it. That means no canned sprinkle cheese in lieu of freshly grated Parmesan. And that a good bottle of olive oil will be well worth the investment. (If you're strapped for cash, here's a trick: Buy a large bottle of affordable olive oil for cooking, and splurge on a small bottle of very high quality for flavoring the finished dish.)

Those outspoken Italians can be the best source for cooking secrets. What have we learned? Telegram from Italy, it's confirmed: Canned tomatoes are A-OK! We've all sampled those large, mealy mid-November tomatoes; and even those fancy, picture-perfect "vine-ripened" ones can fall short on flavor. Real Italians just open a carton of Pomì, and you can bet that every bite is Fellini on a fork. We recommend canned diced tomatoes, and, if you can find them, *pomodorini:* sweet little cherry tomatoes that are often sold in specialty-food markets. Stock up your cabinet for that perfect marinara sauce. Speaking of marinara, when buying fresh basil, why do they give you an entire basil bush? Our friend Lorenzo taught us to freeze leftover fresh basil to throw in that sauce. Another tip: Remove the garlic from the oil before it browns. Unless your recipe calls for it, heat the garlic in the oil and then remove it and throw it away. Burned garlic tastes bitter and will ruin the flavor of the oil, which you'll own two types of and love, right?

When you're finally ready to test your progress, invite an Italian friend over for dinner and keep your eyes peeled for the Universal Gesture of Gastronomic Satisfaction. You'll know you've mastered Italian cooking when you see it: arm bent, hand lifted, palm soft and rotating in circles while the eyes gaze heavenward. When added to that is a sotto voce mutter of *"Mamma mia,"* you'll know that the Pope is clearing a place for you in the Vatican, and that you probably won't have to do the dishes.

PANZANELLA
(BREAD SALAD)

Italians, in their wonderful European way, buy fresh bread every day rather than the processed plastic-wrapped loaves that line American supermarket shelves. This does, however, make for a lot of stale bread. For *panzanella,* which is derived from the Italian word for "little swamp," Italians often soak the bread in water, then squeeze out the water. But because squeezing wet stale bread sounds as appealing to us as a swamp salad, we toast the bread and then let the salad sit a bit to soften it. • *Yield: 4 to 6 servings*

FOR THE SALAD:
5 to 6 slices day-old or fresh bread

1 clove garlic (for rubbing on bread)

4 medium-large ripe tomatoes, cut into 1-inch chunks

1 cucumber, peeled, seeded, and cut into chunks

½ pound fresh mozzarella, cut into cubes

½ small red onion, cut into small pieces

½ cup Kalamata or other brine-cured olives, halved and pitted

½ cup fresh basil leaves, torn into pieces

FOR THE DRESSING:
6 tablespoons olive oil

4 tablespoons red wine vinegar

juice from 1 lemon

1 clove garlic, minced

freshly ground black pepper to taste

salt to taste

1   Rub the slices of bread with the garlic clove, then cut into 1-inch cubes. Toast the bread cubes for a few minutes until browned. Set aside.

2   In a small bowl, whisk together the dressing ingredients.

3   In a large bowl, combine the tomatoes, cucumber, mozzarella, onion, olives, and basil. Add the bread and then the dressing.

4   Stir gently to coat the salad, and let it sit a few minutes before serving to allow the bread to soften.

WE WENT TRADITIONAL HERE, BUT FEEL FREE TO IMPROVISE: MAKE YOUR PANZANELLA WITH WHATEVER FRESH VEGETABLES YOU HAVE ON HAND

RISOTTO WITH TALEGGIO AND PEARS

Taleggio is a soft cow's-milk cheese from the Taleggio Valley, in Northern Italy's Lombardia region. It's also known as a *stracchino,* which is derived from *stracch,* which means "tired" in dialect and refers to the cow's physical (and perhaps emotional) state after grazing in the mountains all summer. Apparently, exhausted cows make great cheese. If you can't find taleggio, fontina can be substituted. From another Italian valley (Valle d'Aosta), fontina is also a soft cheese made from cows, who may or may not be tired; we're not sure. ▪ *Yield: 4 to 6 servings*

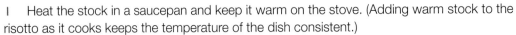

4 cups chicken or vegetable stock
4 tablespoons olive oil
1 small red onion, diced
2 cups arborio rice
2 cups water (this amount may vary)
salt and freshly ground black pepper to taste
¼ pound taleggio cheese, cut into small cubes (about ½ cup)
2 Anjou or Bartlett pears, peeled, cored,
and cut into ½-inch cubes

1   Heat the stock in a saucepan and keep it warm on the stove. (Adding warm stock to the risotto as it cooks keeps the temperature of the dish consistent.)

2   Heat the olive oil in a large saucepan over medium-high heat. Add the onion and stir, cooking until translucent. Reduce the heat slightly, add the rice, and stir to coat with the oil, approximately 1 minute.

3   Add ½ cup of stock and stir the risotto until the stock is absorbed. Continue adding the stock and water ½ cup at a time until all of it is absorbed. This process of adding liquid and stirring should take about 20 minutes, until the rice is al dente.

4   Sprinkle in a dash of salt and pepper, if desired, then add the cheese and pears and stir until the cheese is melted and the pears have softened, approximately 3 minutes. Serve immediately.

RIGATONI ALL'AMATRICIANA

Traditionally, bucatini is used for this recipe, but one CC member described its texture as "wormy," and that was that. This is a quintessentially Roman dish, and Cynthia's friends in Rome insisted that we include it in our Italian chapter and approved the rigatoni substitution. They swear that the parsley garnish is essential, and if you dare substitute Parmesan for the Romano cheese, you risk offending the entire Eternal City. • *Yield: 4 to 6 servings*

2 tablespoons olive oil

1 large onion, diced

1 slice *peperoncino,* or ¼ teaspoon
crushed red pepper flakes

½ pound pancetta, diced (bacon can be substituted)

1 cup white wine

dash freshly ground black pepper

1 28-ounce can diced or peeled tomatoes, undrained

¾ pound rigatoni

¾ cup grated Pecorino Romano cheese

Italian flat-leaf parsley, chopped, for garnish

1   In a large saucepan, heat the olive oil over medium-high heat. Sauté the onion and *peperoncino* slice or red pepper flakes until very golden brown, then remove the onion from the pan and reserve.

2   Add the pancetta to the pan and cook until the edges are brown and crispy, about 15 minutes. Remove the pancetta and drain the fat. Discard the *peperoncino* slice (if using). Return the pancetta and onion to the pan, then add the wine and pepper and simmer until the wine is absorbed.

3   Add the tomatoes and simmer approximately 15 minutes, until the sauce is cooked down.

4   Cook the pasta according to the package directions until al dente, drain, then add the pasta to the sauce. Stir in half of the cheese. Serve with additional grated cheese and garnish with parsley.

PESCE ALL'ACQUA PAZZA
("FISH IN CRAZY WATER")

Anything called "fish in crazy water" deserves a place in our cookbook. Name aside, it's also tasty and light, perfect to follow a heavier risotto or pasta. The small, sweet *branzino* may be the favorite fish for this dish in Italy, but almost any white fish can be substituted; we like snapper, a rather crazy-named fish. • *Yield: 4 to 6 servings*

2 tablespoons olive oil

1 clove garlic, very thinly sliced

4 red snapper fillets (6 to 8 ounces each)

½ cup water

½ cup white wine

1 14-ounce can diced tomatoes, undrained

juice from 1 lemon

1 tablespoon capers

pinch crushed red pepper flakes

¼ cup chopped Italian flat-leaf parsley

salt and freshly ground black pepper to taste

I   In a large nonstick skillet, heat the oil over medium heat. Add the garlic and cook 2 to 3 minutes, until softened.

2   Place the snapper fillets in the skillet skin side down, and combine the remaining ingredients in a bowl and pour over the fillets.

3   Cook the fish over medium-high heat until the sauce begins to boil. Reduce the heat and simmer, covered, 12 to 15 minutes, until the fish is done (opaque). Remove the fish and reduce the sauce for approximately 5 minutes, uncovered. Spoon over the fish and serve immediately.

RICOTTA

BEST QUALITY

RICE BALLS

BROCCOLI RABE
SPINACH BREADS

RICE BREADS

ITALIAN SPECIALTIES
PROSCIUTTO · SOPRSSATA · CAPOCOL

BRUTTI MA BUÒNI ("UGLY BUT GOOD") COOKIES

These cookies may be ugly, but one bite and you'll think yourself too harsh. Which reminds us of a certain mother, who shall remain nameless, who has been known to say, "You know, the ugly ones make the best husbands!" Which makes us think there's a dad out there who deserves some homemade cookies. • *Yield: 4 dozen small cookies*

1 cup blanched almonds
1 cup blanched hazelnuts
1 cup granulated sugar
⅛ teaspoon salt
⅛ teaspoon nutmeg
¼ teaspoon cream of tartar
4 egg whites, brought to room temperature
½ cup confectioners' sugar
½ teaspoon vanilla extract
½ teaspoon almond extract
1 tablespoon cornstarch

1   Preheat the oven to 350 degrees.
2   Toast the almonds and hazelnuts on an ungreased cookie sheet in the oven for 15 minutes or until lightly browned. (Check after 10 minutes to prevent burning.) In a food processor, combine the toasted nuts with the granulated sugar, salt, and nutmeg and chop. (If chopping the nuts by hand, use superfine granulated sugar, to avoid graininess.)
3   In a large bowl, combine the cream of tartar and egg whites. Beat until foamy. Gradually add the confectioners' sugar while beating. Add the vanilla and almond extract. Beat until very soft peaks form. Add the cornstarch and beat until the cornstarch is just blended in. The mixture should look soft, not stiff, and slightly glossy.
4   Gradually fold in the nut mixture with a spatula.
5   Drop by heaping teaspoonfuls onto a cookie sheet lined with parchment paper. Bake for approximately 15 minutes, until just slightly browned.

SGROPPINO
(LEMON DESSERT SHAKE)

In Italy this heavenly drink is often served after fish. Cynthia had it after her first *acqua pazza* on the island of Ponza and swore it was the best thing she had ever tasted. Then again, after half a bottle of wine and a couple of these, she'd probably swear just about anything. • *Yield: 4 servings*

2 cups lemon sorbet
1 cup Prosecco or champagne
¼ cup vodka

Put all the ingredients in a blender and blend on high speed until very creamy and smooth. Pour into champagne glasses and serve immediately.

ITALIAN

A FRENCH 75 COCKTAIL
WITH CC APPETIZERS

party

MENU

MOTT STREET GUACAMOLE

HOMEMADE TORTILLA CHIPS

OPEN-FACED QUESADILLAS

BAKED CHICKEN AND
GOAT CHEESE APPETIZERS

EVERYONE LOVES A CHEESEBALL

THUMBPRINT COOKIES

ABACO PUNCH

FRENCH 75s

drinks are on us

OUR NEAREST AND DEAREST COME CELEBRATE WHAT'S BEEN COOKING

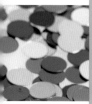

THE PARTY PLANNING BEGINS OVER E-MAIL:

lisa: kitchen goddesses, it's time. i believe cc needs to entertain.

sharon: yes! let's fete ourselves. a self-fete.

becky: great. what should we make?

lucia: cocktails! finally, my forte.

cynthia: simple, festive, delicious little snacks. and maybe a big chicken.

katherine: does this mean we can't wear sweatpants?

becky: no way, let's go semiformal. nothing butters my muffin like seeing my man in a tie.

For us, entertaining in New York City used to mean . . .

1. Calling up a few friends and asking them to meet at the local dive bar for a couple of birthday pops.

2. Having guests over for take-out and a viewing of Joan Rivers's pre-Oscar blow-by-blow on the Red Carpet.

3. Reserving a room at Village Karaoke for a night of bad, loud eighties music.

Let's face it, all of the obstacles standing in the way of throwing a good party make the above options seem like very tempting alternatives. To entertain properly, you need a space roomy enough for mingling, time on your hands to make necessary preparations, and enough food and drink to keep guests from considering skipping out before you unveil dessert. Despite deficiencies of both space and time, Cooking Club has never missed a chance to put our culinary prowess on display.

Our first foray into entertaining took place on a cold winter's night at the inaugural CC Holiday Party. The holidays are a harried time in New York. Between events like the dreaded Office Party and the All-Activity Weekend (when extended family members descend upon the city for body-crushing shopping sprees, fabled Christmas tree–lighting ceremonies, and, inevitably, *The Nutcracker*), the holidays can become just another series of obligations. To take some of the drudgery out of December, we opened up our ovens and our apartments in the name of great entertaining.

Since our first holiday party was such a success, we added an annual summertime gig to the CC calendar. In the course of all of this entertaining, we've discovered that many hands really do make for light work. When you're throwing a party you'll want to arrive early for pre-party primping and decking the halls (think napkin fans, origami, and toothpick Nativity scenes). Also, don't forget: Make more food than usual.

Hors d'oeuvres have come a long way since our moms' hostessing heydays. And since this isn't your mother's cookbook, you won't find separate entries for "Easy Cheeseball" and "Cocktail Cheeseball," which are not to be confused with the "Cheese Puff" or the "Cheese Whizzer." Instead, we offer one recipe, which we've dubbed Everyone Loves a Cheeseball. Some of our other party favorites include a tangy guacamole with fresh tomato that has been the go-to dip at almost every Cooking Club party. We're also sharing our secret for Homemade Tortilla Chips. Next up is a little baked chicken and goat cheese number that originated as an entrée. We liked it so much, we miniaturized it so that we could serve it at one of our soirees. Also in the apps category is the Open-Faced Quesadilla, an endlessly versatile recipe for a fresh-veggie-and-jack-cheese combination that's to die for.

In the Wonderfully Festive Party Beverage category, we've got a couple of winners. The first concoction is a Caribbean rum drink discovered in the Abaco Islands of the Bahamas. The perfect party drink, Abaco Punch is light, not too sweet, and sanctioned by our own Liquid Pleasure Director. If rum's not your game, we've got a classic champagne cocktail called the French 75. One caveat: Encourage guests to sample some of our wickedly tasty shortbread cookies before too many trips to the punch bowl.

MOTT STREET GUACAMOLE

Many dishes that Lucia brought to our table—at least in the early days—were inspired by her college roommate Georgia Close, a.k.a. "The Source." In the face of a culinary conundrum, Lucia used to crumble like a hunk of feta and press 1 on her speed dial for a fail-safe recipe. This is one of them. And it's easy enough to pass off as your own. . . . • *Yield: 8 to 10 servings (about 2 cups)*

2 large ripe avocados, peeled and pitted
1 tomato, seeded and diced
½ red onion, diced
½ cup finely chopped cilantro
¼ teaspoon cayenne pepper
¼ teaspoon ground cumin
salt and freshly ground black pepper to taste
juice from 1 lime

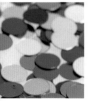

Mash up the avocados with a fork. Add the vegetables, cilantro, and spices. Squeeze in lime juice to taste.

HOMEMADE TORTILLA CHIPS

It doesn't get any more Martha than this, ladies. Yes, it's a sweaty affair, and you'll wind up splattered in scalding-hot oil, but the wounds will be worth it when you roll out your basket of custom-made chips. We made heart-shaped ones at a sexy foods night, but any shape is possible with a paring knife and a little imagination. Christmas cookie cutters, by the way, are a no-brainer here. • *Yield: 10 servings (about 50 chips)*

1 2-dozen package corn tortillas
vegetable oil
(copious amounts of) salt

1   Cut the tortillas into desired shapes.
2   Pour about half an inch of the oil into a large, deep skillet. Turn the heat up to high. When the oil is very hot, carefully drop 3 to 4 tortillas into it at a time. Cook for about 5 to 10 seconds per side, or until golden brown. Remove them from the oil and place on paper towels to remove excess grease. Salt them, and let them cool and harden before serving.

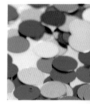

PARTY

OPEN-FACED QUESADILLAS

Who hasn't been here before: standing before a cavernously empty cupboard, scrutinizing the miserable lineup of canned goods that have quite possibly rusted to the cabinet shelf? It was during one of these bleak moments that Lucia started opening cans and improvising. Lucky for us, this recipe is a far cry from its prototype, which literally couldn't boast a single noncanned ingredient. • *Yield: 10 to 12 servings (6 quesadillas)*

1 large red pepper, diced
1 large yellow pepper, diced
1 large orange pepper, diced
1 large tomato, diced
1 red onion, diced
1 15½-ounce can whole kernel corn (no salt), strained
1 15½-ounce can black beans, rinsed and strained
juice from ½ lime
juice from ½ lemon
2 teaspoons olive oil
2 teaspoons red wine vinegar
salt and freshly ground black pepper to taste
6 slices mountain bread (or flour tortillas)
2 cups shredded pepper jack cheese

1   Preheat the oven to 350 degrees.
2   In a large mixing bowl, combine all the vegetables and the beans. Add the lime juice, lemon juice, olive oil, vinegar, salt, and pepper. (If you go no further, you'll have an excellent summertime bean salad.)
3   Pour into a skillet and cook over low heat for 10 minutes, stirring occasionally, until warm. Remove from the heat.
4   Meanwhile, warm the bread in the oven for 10 minutes.
5   Spoon the vegetable mixture over the bread so that it covers it entirely. Sprinkle with the cheese. Put back in the oven for 10 more minutes, until the cheese is melted, being careful not to let the edges overcook. Cut the quesadillas into triangles and serve hot.

BAKED CHICKEN AND
GOAT CHEESE APPETIZERS

In another life, these tasty little morsels were an entrée in their own right. We've made them bite-size so that we can serve them at parties, but it's easy enough to use a whole chicken breast for a stick-to-your-ribs kind of dinner. Also, while we swear by goat cheese, mozzarella is a great, melty option. • *Yield: 12 appetizers*

2 tablespoons unsalted butter

1½ pounds chicken strips (or tenders), cleaned,
trimmed of fat, and pounded to ¼-inch thickness

salt and freshly ground black pepper to taste

1 12-ounce package goat cheese

1 cup flour

2 eggs, beaten

1 cup plain breadcrumbs

¼ cup dried rosemary

1 tablespoon dried thyme

¼ cup dried basil

¾ cup white wine

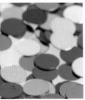

1   Preheat the oven to 350 degrees.

2   Melt the butter and brush both sides of the chicken lightly with it. Sprinkle with salt and pepper. Spread 1 to 2 tablespoons of goat cheese onto each chicken strip. Roll up and fasten with toothpicks.

3   Organize 3 dishes: one for the flour, one for the eggs, and one for the breadcrumbs combined with the spices. Roll the chicken roll-ups in flour first, then dip in the eggs, and then roll in the breadcrumb mixture.

4   Arrange in a greased baking dish, and sprinkle any leftover breadcrumbs on top. Bake for 25 minutes. Pour the wine over the entire dish and bake for another 5 to 10 minutes.

EVERYONE LOVES A CHEESEBALL

This is an easy recipe for a real crowd-pleasing hors d'oeuvre. If you're throwing a holiday party, forget the gingerbread men; try sculpting a cheeseball snowman instead. Finely chopped walnuts or chopped olives can be substituted for the sesame seeds. • *Yield: about 2 dozen*

1 8-ounce package cream cheese, softened
2 cups shredded Cheddar cheese
2 tablespoons olive oil
1 tablespoon red wine vinegar
2 tablespoons dry sherry
1 teaspoon soy sauce
½ teaspoon dry mustard
¼ cup sesame seeds, toasted

1   In a medium mixing bowl, combine all the ingredients except the sesame seeds and blend well. Cover and refrigerate for about 2 hours, until firm.

2   Toast the sesame seeds in a 350-degree oven until golden brown, about 3 to 4 minutes.

3   Let the seeds cool and put them in a small bowl.

4   Form the mixture into 1-inch balls (or smaller, if you prefer). Roll the balls in the sesame seeds and place on a tray. Cover and refrigerate for at least 30 minutes.

PARTY

CHAMPAGNE AND
A PLATEFUL OF
THUMBPRINT
COOKIES MAKE
BECKY (LEFT)
AND LISA VERY
HAPPY INDEED

THUMBPRINT COOKIES

This recipe for shortbread cookies is virtually foolproof. And it's no wonder: It's an age-old home-ec teacher's staple. Plus you get to use your hands a lot, which is always a bonus. Use any kind of jam you like to fill the centers. We like raspberry. Or you can try different flavors for a colorful display. • *Yield: 3 dozen*

3 cups sifted flour
½ cup sugar
½ pound (2 sticks) unsalted butter, softened
1 egg yolk
fruit jam

1   Preheat the oven to 350 degrees. Grease a cookie sheet and set it aside.
2   Mix the first 3 ingredients with clean hands. Add the egg yolk, and knead well.
3   Form the dough into balls about the size of a grape. Place the balls on the prepared cookie sheet. Press the center of each ball with your thumb to create a well for the jam.
4   Bake until golden brown, about 10 to 15 minutes. Remove from the oven. When fully cooled, fill the centers with jam.

PARTY

ABACO PUNCH

This concoction is lighter than a piña colada and more refreshing than your typical rum punch; one sip and you'll swear you're beachside in the tropical sun. The guidelines below are but a mere sketch—the real pleasure in this potion lies in mastering the ideal mix while flanked by a team of worthy testing lieutenants. Cheers! • *Yield: 1½ quarts*

1 cup dark rum
1 cup coconut rum
¼ cup apricot brandy
2 cups pineapple juice
3 cups grapefruit juice
juice from 1 lime
ice
lime slices, for garnish (1 per glass)

In a large pitcher, combine all the ingredients. Stir well. Garnish with slices of lime if desired. Mini drink umbrellas are optional.

FRENCH 75s

Legend has it, this classic champagne cocktail packs the same kick as a World War I seventy-five-millimeter French cannon. Yowza. • *Yield: 1 serving*

3 parts champagne
1 part brandy
fresh strawberries, for garnish
sugar, for garnish

Mix the champagne and brandy in a champagne flute. For an elegant garnish, slice the strawberries vertically down the middle (leaving the tops intact), roll in the sugar, and place on the rims of champagne flutes before serving.

WHAT'S ON THE COOKING CLUB HORIZON? BECKY (LEFT) AND CYNTHIA LOOK FORWARD TO NEXT YEAR. . . .

Index

THE COOKING CLUB

Katherine Fausset, a literary agent, hails straight from Cajun Country. This hot tamale is the keeper of many an age-old bayou secret recipe, including a delectable Bananas Foster, the closest thing we've experienced to heaven. Katherine has also been dubbed, albeit unwittingly, Aphrodisiac Queen, thanks to her oyster quiche, which left its indelible mark on the club in the form of our Sex and the Kitchen night. She has no doubt that using one stick of butter instead of two makes a recipe low-fat.

Sharon Cohen Fredman, a print production director, is the healthy conscience of the Cooking Club. Reigning impresario of the low-fat dessert, Sharon keeps us fitting into our aprons. Sharon also acts as Roving Club Correspondent by culling recipes from exotic ports-of-call, such as Sydney, the Loire Valley, and central Jersey. She believes that the way to her husband's heart is by making him sit home alone and hungry on the first Sunday of each month.

Rebecca Sample Gerstung, a magazine editor, has been known to open up a fresh can of whoop-ass for dinner. Becky's secret ingredient, her signature sass, never fails to stir up a little excitement at Sunday dinners. The fearless champion of red meat in the CC repertoire and the mastermind behind comfort food night, this Midwestern miss likes to serve all her dishes with a side of bacon.

An art director and self-proclaimed Cooking Club president, **Cynthia Harris** has been oft described as the "glue that holds the club together." As a designer, Cynthia pays compulsive attention to aesthetics in her creations, and has been caught carving lady apples into votive candleholders deep into the night. Chef Cyn, as she's known to the Club, spent more than a few sleepless nights designing this book and, it should be noted, owns her own glue gun.

Lucia Quartararo, a book editor, is known as the fastest draw in Cooking Club due to a couple of infamous and not-soon-forgotten culinary gaffes, like pumpkin-pie filling from a can and store-bought eggnog. Despite recent efforts, most of her memorable creations have been in the beverage category, earning her the title of Liquid Pleasure Director. When in culinary doubt, she adds goat cheese.

Magazine editor **Lisa Singer** is the only member who chose her apartment based on its proximity to fresh produce. While sometimes intimidating to fellow members with her high standards of culinary excellence and her insistence on gastronomic political correctness (swordfish bad, salmon good), she has raised the bar for her clubmates. She also knows how to use the food processor both to julienne and to puree.